Walking the Alps from Mediterranean to Adriatic

Ian C M MacLennan

Copyright © 2014 Ian C M MacLennan

All rights reserved.

ISBN:1500705381

ISBN-13: 978-1500705381

DEDICATION

To those who love the freedom of the hills.

CONTENTS

	Acknowledgments	i
	Prologue: The Birth of a Concept	1
1	Chapter: Menton to Briançon	5
2	Chapter: Briançon to St Gingolph	37
3	Chapter: St Gingolph to Meiringen	69
4	Chapter: Meiringen to Pontresina	95
5	Chapter: Pontresina to Niederdorf	121
6	Chapter: Niederdorf to Vitorio Veneto	151
	Appendices	179
	i When to walk	179
	ii Mapping	179
	iii Points of entry and exit	181
	iv Finding and booking accommodation	182
	v Equipment	183
	Index	185

ACKNOWLEDGMENTS

Firstly I thank my walking companions. John Simmons completed the entire walk with me, while John Delamere walked from Menton to Vella and again from Niederdorf to Vittorio Veneto. John Milles shared the first 5 days from Menton and then the continuous walk from Briançon to Pontresina. Andrew MacLennan walked with us for a week of each of the first five years and Michael Reth joined us from the Refuge de la Golèse to St Gingolph at the end of the second year. Their companionship on the walk enormously increased the enjoyment of this adventure and they have kindly allowed me to use some of their photographs.

I am indebted to John Delamere and my wife Pam for proof reading the manuscript and for many helpful suggestions. The walk could not have continued after the first 30 days if Andrew Thomas and his team at the Royal Orthopaedic Hospital in Birmingham, had not successfully resurfaced my left hip.

For most of the walk our wives and partners have patiently waited for us at home, although Pam, Anne and Helen came to Venice to celebrate with us at the end of the walk. In addition Pam and Anne met us at our lodgings from the Auener Hoff to Niederdorf during the fifth year of our traverse of the Alps.

Google searches and Google Earth have been used in planning the route and finding accommodation. Through France we have used IGN 1:25k maps of "les Alpes" and "Provence, Côte d'Azure, Mediterranée et Corse" www.memory-map.co.uk. In Switzerland we walked using "Swiss Mobility" maps and software http://map.wanderland.ch/. Hard copies of 1:25k Tabacco Maps were used for navigation in the Südtyrol and Veneto Dolomites. The web site "Walking and Hiking in the Südtyrol" has been invaluable for planning walks in this Italian province www.trekking.suedtirol.info/. The Amazon CreateSpace web site https://www.createspace.com/Products/Book/ has helped convert this concept to the printed book.

Finally I thank the wonderful people who accommodated and fed us in mountain huts and other lodgings throughout our walk through the Alps.

ICMM 07.07.2014.

PROLOGUE
THE BIRTH OF A CONCEPT

John Simmons (JS) and I began our joint climbing ventures in 1990. I had never previously climbed outside Europe, while John had been to the Himalaya and Andes several times. Despite this disparity in experience, as the only climbing members aged over fifty on an expedition to Aconcagua we decided to pair up for our climb to the summit. The expedition was organized by the BMRES (Birmingham Medical Research Expeditionary Society) and included a series of scientific experiments on the participants at 9,000, 14,000 and 18,000ft before we were free to go for the 22,837ft summit. Since then we have been on a number of other excursions with the BMRES in the Alps, Andes and Himalaya.

By 2006, although neither of us had stopped working, we were over 65 and had shelved a number of responsibilities. This made it realistic to think of engaging in some extended walks in the European Alps. A preliminary outing in the Vanoise, included a circular walk to the Arc valley and back from Pralongan. The following year we took on a more ambitious project, walking 303km from Die in the Drôme through the Vercors, Dévoluy, Écrins and Queyras Alps to Briançon. This tremendous excursion showed us that multiday walks without rest days are practicable, if suitably-spaced lodgings that provide meals can be found.

Unsurprisingly, we decided to follow up this journey across the Southern Alps with another long walk. The ancient fortified town and citadel of Briançon had been an excellent place to finish in 2007. It is an attractive and bustling place in the heart of the French Alps that has a good rail service to the TGV stations and airports at Marseille and

Lyon. With this in mind a suitable sequel seemed to be a walk from the Mediterranean coast to Briançon along the Italian-French border.

The classical long distance path between the Mediterranean through Briançon is GR5. This starts from Nice and heads north through the sprawling suburbs to the east of the river Var, bypassing much of the Alps Maritime. Our preference was to start at Menton and for the first 5 days walk over the border hills following the more challenging GR52 with some variants. After this our route used a series of unclassified paths on either side of the international border for 8 days before finally linking with GR5 for the last 2 days into Briançon.

When we set out from Menton our thoughts were only on the walk to Briançon. We had no plans to continue further north, let alone to undertake a full traverse of the Alps. This idea evolved as we made our way through the hills. We first extended the walk to Lake Geneva. Then it was inevitable that we would continue through Switzerland and the Eastern Italian Alps to Vittorio-Veneto, where the high hills fall to the Venetian plain.

On these walks we have found magnificent solitude, for where possible we have selected routes that are off the beaten track. Also we follow the BMRES tradition of going at our own pace and so often walk alone. In the evenings, on the other hand, we found plenty to talk about at our lodgings, where we have invariably met interesting and friendly people.

By the time we were ready to set off to the South of France three other members of the BMRES asked to join us. John Delamere (JD), John Milles (JM), and my son Andrew. They have walked with us for large sections of our traverse of the Alps.

This log of our 82-day walk from Menton to Vittorio-Veneto is designed to include sufficient detail for a reader to be able to walk our route in manageable stages and find accommodation and board each night. The Kindle version can be carried as a guide. Hopefully it will convey some of the delights experienced on our way through the Alps.

The walk does not coincide with any of the Via Alpina trails www.via-alpina.org/en/, but occasionally joins GR5 and the Swiss Via Alpina. Otherwise it is off the long distance tracks and finds solitude in the magnificent mountain scenery. To complete the walk it is necessary to be able to navigate in the high hills and have a good head for heights. Often the paths are not smooth, sometimes they are exposed and in places are non-existent. A degree of fitness is necessary, but JS and I still enjoy these walks in our mid seventies and are continuing on further long walks in the hills.

The six walks between Mediterranean and Adriatic

Menton to Briançon, 14-28 June 2008
263km, 22,619m ascent

Briançon to St Gingolph, 22 June-7 July 2009
294km, 22,366m ascent

St Gingolph to Meiringen, 2-13 September 2010
199km, 14,075m ascent

Meiringen to Pontresina, 25 June-8 July 2011
262km, 17,185m ascent

Pontresina to Niederdorf, 7-22 September 2012
302km, 17,047m ascent

Niederdorf to Vittorio Veneto, 6-16 September 2013
180km, 12,230m ascent

Total 1,500 km and 106 km ascent in 82 days
averaging 18.3km and 1,287m ascent per day

Day 7 on the French Italian border ridge at the Tête Rougnouse de la Guercha

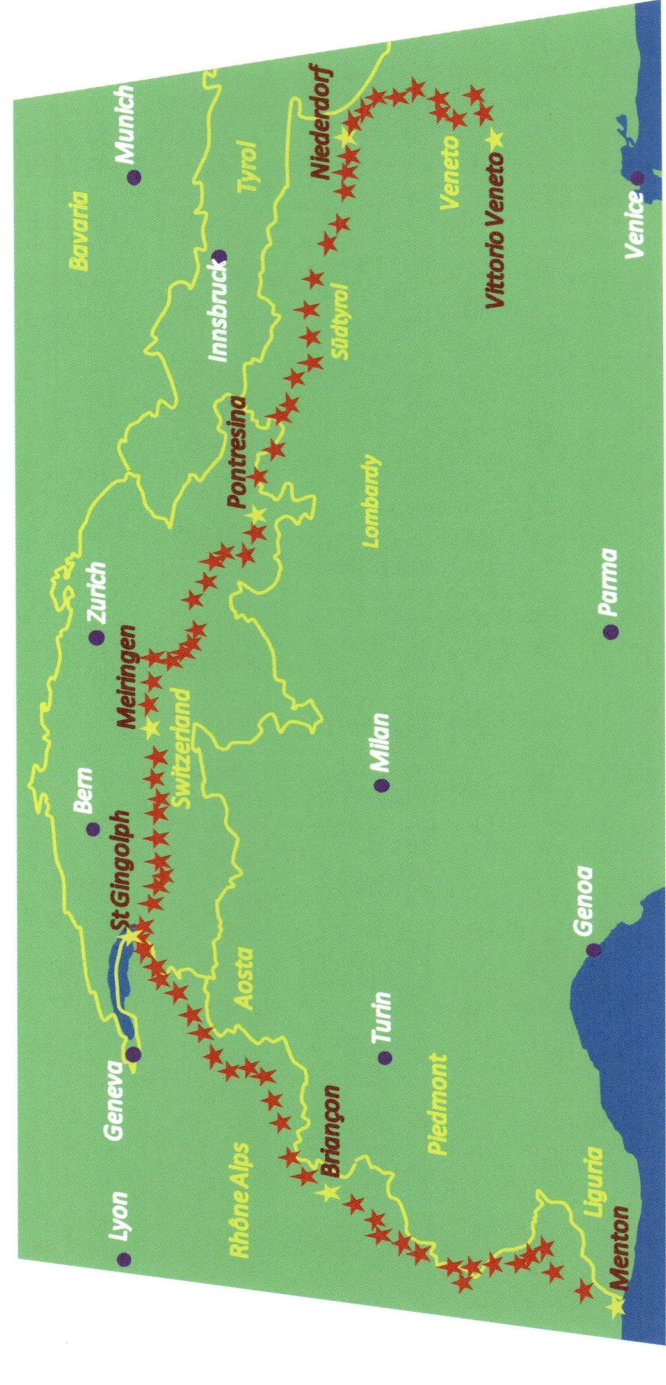

The 82-day walk from Menton to Vittorio-Vento

The red and yellow stars mark the 82 stopovers on our traverse of the Alps, the yellow stars indicating the starts and finishes of each year's walk. Yellow lines show international borders

1 CHAPTER
DAYS 1-15 MENTON TO BRIAÇON
A walk from the Mediterranean among the French-Italian border hills

Journey to Menton on the Côte d'Azure

As our flight approached Nice the sun shone over the Mediterranean, but menacing clouds covered the Maritime Alps. Happily the greyness over the hills was the last of weeks of bad weather with heavy snowfall at altitude. We were going to enjoy many days of sunshine over the next fifteen days on our walk to Briançon.

A train from Nice Central took us to Menton, going through a series of tunnels in the limestone hills that extend along the Côte d'Azure. Menton is a quiet place of unpretentious style. Its location just before the Italian border is an ideal starting point for a traverse of the Alps. The hills rise steeply behind the railway line (page 7) preventing the sprawling suburbs that characterize its large neighbour - Nice. It was a mere two minute walk from the station to our lodgings, the Hotel Modern www.hotel-moderne-menton.com, and not longer from there to the sea. The price and name of this hotel had led us to suspect we were staying in basic accommodation. Consequently, we walked straight past the Modern, not realizing that that this fine building was our hotel. Once inside our rooms were found to be comfortable and well cooled. The balconies were just the place to relax after the journey.

We wandered down to the shore and from the point between the Menton and Garvan bays looked up at the hills we were to enter the following day (page 7). Clearly we were going to be getting straight into mountains. It seemed that Menton was going to be an excellent place to start our long walk and the next day proved this conclusion correct.

Days 1-15 Menton to Briançon

Day 1: Menton to Sospel (420m)
18.3 km, ascent 1820m, descent 1454m, 7h30
High point the Colla Bassa 1110m

We made our way past the elegant houses of a pedestrianized street stopping briefly to buy bread and fruit for lunch. This led to the next bay and it was then a short walk along the front to Garvan yacht harbour. Just before Menton Garvan railway station a side road led to the narrow steep alley that marks the start of GR52. The high walls that flank the first part of the route provided welcome shade from the bright morning sun as we made our way upwards along successive passageways. Soon we passed under a pedestal-carried section of the autoroute (below) that protects the coastal towns from through traffic. Now the buildings petered out and we could see west to Monte Carlo and follow the white trails of speeding boats cutting through the vivid blue surface of the bay. After the autoroute we continued on a zigzagging path, climbing steeply up the floral, shrub-covered and fragrant hillside. Seven hundred meters above the sea there is a short respite in the climb where the path crosses a relatively flat meadow, the Plan de Lyon.

JS and JD with Garvin Harbour in the Background

7

To the right at the far side of the meadow two limestone buttresses rise to the first high pass. We climbed in the gully between these buttresses on a steep path that winds back and forth across coarse limestone scree and leads to the Col du Berceau. This picturesque, pine-shaded grassy platform is a great place to rest. The foreshortened view down to Menton (below) gave the impression we could toss pebbles into the sea. We had climbed nearly 1,100m in 3.5 horizontal km from Garvan harbour, a magnificent start to our long walk.

From this first col we descended on thinly-wooded hillside to a ruined castelet, losing some 300 metres. As we passed to the northeast of the ruins there was a large flock of noisily baaing sheep. Now the route headed northwards climbing gradually on a stony track to the Colla Bassa. From there a largely horizontal path traverses to the third pass, the Col de Razet. At this col we found the first of the numbered signposts [90] that characterize the Alps Maritime. The position of these useful navigation aids is shown by their boxed number on the 1:25,000 IGN maps. We rested here for a few minutes before starting the gentle 5km descent, mainly through woods, to the ancient town of Sospel. At the mid-point of the descent there is a slight rise to a clearing in the woods where there is a stone water trough. Soon after this, at signpost [107], the path veers to the northwest and descends to a broad track that leads to the metalled D2566 road at a hairpin bend.

Instead of following GR52 down the road to Sospel we went uphill in the direction of the Col de Chastillon. The Auberge Provençal www.aubergeprovencale.fr/ where we spent the night lies at the apex of the second hairpin bend, marked [106] on the map. This two-star Logis Hotel has a scenic terrace overlooking Sospel. The food was good, but their bottled beer seriously over-priced. Unfortunately we only found this out when we had each greedily consumed the contents of 3 small bottles to quench our thirst after this strenuous, but memorable, first day under the Provençal sun.

Day 2: Sospel to Baisse de Camp d'Argent (1743m)
21.5 km, ascent 2,423m, descent 1100m, 8h45
High point Mont Giagiabella 1902m

Although there is considerable ascent on the way to the Baisse de Camp d'Argent we found this walk perfectly manageable. Baisse is a synonym for the French words col and pas. It is used in the southern Alps d'Haut Provence and Alps Maritime, but ceases to appear north of the Tinée valley. Although the word probably relates to the French verb – baisser, to lower its usage seems to be Occitan. I wonder if it has any etymological link to the Gaelic word for a col – bealach, or the equivalent Welsh bwlch.

The day's route follows GR52 as it climbs to a ridge rising in 12 km from 300m in the old town of Sospel to 1900m and then continues, undulating at around this height for another 8km to the Authion. This hill marks the convergence of several ridges and has been considered to be of great strategic importance. It supports a series of now-ruined hill-top forts and barracks that were involved in battles in Napoleonic times. These forts were also used by the occupying forces in the 1939-45 war and were liberated at great cost by the first division of the Free French Army in a heroic, but seemingly unwise, attack with terrible loss of life. On 11 and 12 April 1945, less than a month before peace was declared in Europe, a bloody battle was fought in which 276 Free-French soldiers were killed.

The walk starts down the D2566 from the hotel for a few yards and then takes a path descending to the right that crosses the road twice and then the railway before reaching a road junction at signpost [105]. From there the route heads nor-nor-west through the southern outskirts of Sospel passing over a small stream before reaching the river Bévéra. Here we turned left along the river bank to the ancient stone bridge (previous page) that leads to the old town of Sospel. This bridge has an impressive fortified gateway and there is a stone plaque in the

wall to the left of the bridge that indicates Menton in one direction and Merveilles in the other. On the far side of the bridge we crossed an attractive square, leaving this from the left side and sequentially passing signposts [71] and [74] on the road leading northwest out of the town. At [74] GR52 becomes a well-made mule track that allows rapid progress at the start of the ascent (above). After climbing some 250m there is a short section on a country road until signpost [75], from where the path heads northwest crossing another lane at [76] before climbing a fine ridge to reach the Baisse de Liniere at 1342m, already a thousand metres above Sospel.

At this pleasant grassy col a large rusted artillery piece lies in the grass; a remnant of ancient defences that are found at several places along this border route through the Maritime Alps. The barrel provided a comfortable seat for a short break in the morning sun. The path splits at the col and we followed GR52 to the right. This continues on the ridge for a while before veering onto its western flank. The next two tops– the Chime du Ters and the Mangiabo – are avoided as the path skirts round their western ridges. The main crête is rejoined temporarily at signpost [143] before the path traverses once more onto the hillside of the west flank of the Cime de la Gonella. Red dots on the map suggest the traverse here is delicate. In the event although the slope is steep the path is well-made and only caused problems because it was very muddy. We learnt later that this mud was due to 360 fell-runners who had been racing down the route in the rain on the previous day. We did well to miss them, for it would not have been easy to pass on the path. The variation in weather in this region was apparent, for while we had enjoyed sunshine the previous day it had been raining in these higher hills.

The mud ended at the Baisse de la Déa [141], where the path crosses a rough mountain track. Our main climb of the day was now over, but the bright sun of the morning had gone and we ate our sandwiches in mist with a flock of sheep for company. After lunch we continued for a km or so on the east flank of the Pointe de Ventabren (1978m) before reaching another col and the same mountain track that we had crossed earlier. On the far side of this track the GR deviates to the more gentle west slope of the ridge and continues above the track for another 4 km before joining the metalled D68 mountain road at a hairpin bend. Here we left GR52, as this goes straight on to the Authion, where the lodging is only for spirits of the departed. We followed the road downhill through another hairpin to a right-hand bend, where there is a vacherie below the road. Our route heads east from here just below and parallel to the road. At the start this is a track that later becomes a path. It is waymarked with yellow flashes and is shown as black dashes on the map. It contours the hillside below the road, which it eventually rejoins at the Baisse de Camp d'Argent. Another path, also marked with yellow flashes, descends from the Vacherie and must be avoided.

On arriving at the Baisse de Camp d'Argent we turned right to the gîte d'étape "L'Estive du Mercantour", www.estive-mercantour.fr/.

This is an excellent lodging house, where we were given a very warm welcome. We sat round an open fire drying out after the mist of the afternoon.

Day 3: Camp d'Argent to Ref des Merveilles (2115m)
12.8km, ascent 1237m, descent 850m, 5h00
High point le Pas du Diable 2432m

The murky weather of the previous evening had cleared and there was bright sunshine as we said goodbye to our generous hosts. The grassy ski run opposite the gîte led us over the Chime de Tuis before descending to a war memorial beside the road at [244]. In retrospect it would be quicker and still pleasant to walk up the road from the gîte to the memorial.

GR52a climbs from the memorial to the crest of the grassy west ridge of the Authion, which it follows for a km to the west summit of the hill. The slopes were covered in early summer flowers including cowslips and orchids, but most poignant were the huge drifts of white Pasque Flower Anemones (above), a reminder of the useless slaughter of young men that had occurred on this hillside 53 years before.

From the west summit of the Authion the view north looks along a winding ridge that ends in the Chime du Diable with our target the Pas du Diable on its eastern flank (below). We headed north from this summit and then west-nor-west along a broad ridge. Ahead lay an ancient and artillery-damaged square fortress. Just before and below this tower at signpost [410] we rejoined GR52 on a track that descends northwards on the west side of the ridge to the Baisse de St. Véran [409]. There we met a shepherd with his two Border Collies, who told us that it had rained almost every day for the previous six weeks and that he was enjoying the rare sunshine. It was these weeks of rain that translated into the exceptional snow cover we were to encounter later in the day and at high level throughout the Alps Maritimes. From the baisse de St. Véran GR52 continues on the east side of the ridge as a path, climbing sharply to the Col de Raus. The path then crosses the ridge and passes onto the steep north-eastern flank of the Cime de Raus, where it traverses to the Baisse de Caveline (2107m). Several chamois were grazing at this col. These graceful animals have become

remarkably tame in the Mercantour National Park, where hunting is prohibited. The path from the Baisse de Caveline traverses east, descending some 30m to the floor of the valley and then climbing on its far side to the Pas du Diable, our high point of the day. As we made our way between rocks we started to cross patches of snow and the snow had become continuous when we reached the pass.

From the pass we walked on compass baring 336° across the snow for 0.25km to a point [404] between the two small frozen Lacs du

Diable before turning to the east making our way between boulders to the north of the Lac de la Muta. After next passing south of the Lac du Trem we finally descended southeast of the Lac Fourca to the Refuge des Merveilles www.cafnice.org/site/refuge/merveilles/. This CAF refuge offers dormitory accommodation with multi-birth bunks, good food and cold showers. In June 2008 we found this to be an efficiently managed refuge, but it was run rather strictly. For example, access to the dormitories and inside toilets was denied until 6 pm.

Day 4: Ref des Merveilles to la Madone de Fenestre (1903m)
16km, ascent 1450m, descent 1678m, 6h30
High point le Pas de l'Arpette 2511m

Local advice suggested that the long high route followed by GR52 would be impracticable to complete in a day with the prevailing snow conditions. I needed no persuading about this, for it had been a challenging walk with steep approaches on each side of the 3 successive cols, when I had gone that way on a fine day in September 2002. Fortunately there is an alternative route that runs south of GR52.

We set off on this southern option climbing more or less due west from the refuge to the Pas de l'Arpette. It was overcast at the col, but the clouds gradually cleared as we descended westwards, crossing a number of snow-filled gullies, before reaching the floor of the hanging Val d'Empuonrame. From the mouth of this upper valley a steep zigzagging path winds down wooded hillside to the D171 road-head at the Pont du Countet. Again we saw several chamois on the descent (opposite). Some 1.5km down the mountain road we stopped at the Relais de Merveilles. This pleasant gîte provided us with large sandwiches and coffee. It looked as though this would be a good place on a future walk to spend a night.

After this break we continued down the road to [275] and then began a steep zigzagging ascent northwest up open hillside, gaining some 800m before reaching a ridge northeast of the Baisse de Prais. From there we could see the rock aiguilles that rise to the east of the Madone de Fenestre moodily surrounded in cloud (below). We took a path marked with black dashes on the map that descends and then

traverses north to a hanging valley with its five Lacs de Prals. At the far northern side of the lakes a path climbs to the Baisse de Cinq Lacs. Here we were greeted by lightening rapidly followed by thunder, giving impetus to our descent of the Vallon du Ponset to the northeast. The Chapel and CAF Refuge at la Madone de Fenestre were already in view as the rain started. We ran the last couple of hundred meters and managed to scurry into the refuge without getting soaked. This was the only rain we were to experience on the whole of our walk between Menton and Briançon.

There was a warm welcome from the guardian of this large refuge www.cafnice.org/site/refuge/madone/. We were immediately shown to our room, which we had to ourselves. This was furnished with 4 two-tier bunks. There were hot showers and we changed into dry clothes before descending for a welcome beer in the dining room. The food and wine were good and the atmosphere relaxed and convivial, happily contrasting with the severity of the welcome of previous evening. The attractive cluster of buildings that include the refuge originally housed a monastery, founded in the 12th century by monks of the Benedictine order. It is worth spending a little time visiting the almost cave-like Chapel by the Refuge.

Day 5: la Madone de Fenestre to le Boréon (1530m)
13.4km, ascent 1070m, descent 1474m, 5hr15
High point the Chime de Piagu 2338m

After the overnight storm it was a brilliant cloudless morning, heralding the near perfect weather we were to enjoy for the rest of our walk to Briançon. In these conditions the day's relatively short walk is interesting and varied and provides stunning views of the high peaks of the Alps Maritime.

There was still frost on the ground as we headed west from the refuge, climbing to the ridge that separates the valley of la Madone de Fenestre from that of le Boréon. This relatively easy path leads in 3 km

up open hillside to the Chime du Pisset (2233m), the first summit on the ridge. The crystal clear view from there opened up to the high Border hills with their peppering of fresh snow gleaming in the morning sun (opposite). The cool air was wonderfully refreshing.

It was another 3 km to the high point of the ridge, the Cime de Piagu, with a short but steep pull up the last section to the summit. From here the path, marked with yellow flashes, descends a fine ridge to the southwest (below). Some 550m below the Cime de Piagu and after the ridge becomes forested we took a right fork at signpost [385]. This path traverses back north and then northwest on the Boréon side of the hill and is also marked with yellow flashes. It is an entertaining route and no gentle walk in the woods, for several fallen trees had to be

negotiated and in places there were significant ascents and descents to avoid rocky outcrops. At signpost [383], a point north of and some 560m below the Cime de Piagu, we took a left fork and headed down through the forest to the road at le Boréon.

The gîte d'étape du Boréon http://giteduboreon.monsite-orange.fr/ lies a little way up a lane to the right off the road that leads to the Col Salèse. We arrived at the gîte at 13.30. As the family were eating Sunday lunch they politely asked if we would come back later. Fortunately the weather was still fine and we found a pleasant restaurant with a terrace down the hill by the Lac du Boréon. Although it was already 14.00 they were happy to serve us delicious grilled trout with Provençal rosé, making the wait for the gîte to open a pleasure rather than a bore.

Day 6: Le Boréon to Isola 2000 (2050m)
20.2km, ascent 1644m, descent 1112m, 7hr15
High point the the Tête Mercière 2491m

We followed GR52 to the Col Salèse, going west from the gîte on the road for 1.7km to signpost [399], where we descended to the left on a path through the forest to the Boréon Torrent. After crossing this stream by a wooden bridge GR52 continues along the far bank and then climbs gently through the woods. As we approached the col the spring flowers on the forest floor included exquisite vivid dark blue

gentians. Sadly when we reached the Col Salèse JM and Andrew had to leave us to return to work. They were to climb south over Mont Archas on their way to St Martin Vesubie, where they got a bus to Nice airport.

The three pensioners – JS, JD and myself continued west following the red and white GR52 waymarks for about half a km before reaching [267]. There we left GR52 for the last time, taking a track to the right that crosses the valley stream by the Pont d'Ingolf and contours on the north side of the valley at about 2000m. This pleasant and often grassy track continues for 6km through larch forest. The needles of the well-spaced trees were still the innocent green of late spring, providing a wonderful filter for the light from the clear blue sky. At [256] the path starts to ascend in long loops in a generally north-westerly direction, passing some well-preserved military bunkers set into the hillside below the Col de Mercière.

We decided to make a detour from the main path at the bunkers and climb westwards across the alp to the high point on the ridge, the Tête Mercière (2491m). Our view to the east looked towards the border hills (opposite) while below us to the north lay the ski resort Isola 2000 (below). On the far side of this valley we could see the border ridge, which was to give us such delectable walking the following day.

Until 1945 the high valley holding Isola 2000 was an Italian, royal hunting ground. This was ceded to the French at the end of hostilities. It was then a summer pasture until the ski station was built through the entrepreneurial initiative of a British Army officer - Peter Boumphrey. The resort was opened in 1971. Isola 2000 lies 1120m above and 15km from the small ancient village of Isola, which lies on the north bank of the Tinée River.

From our view-point we descended east to the Col Mercière [95] and then headed down into the Isola 2000 resort, passing a small reservoir before reaching the high-rise holiday apartment blocks. At the end of a long line of these buildings we came to an office at a roundabout where we picked up the keys for the night's accommodation. This had been arranged through a local estate agent at the Agence de Colombe www.decolombe.com/. Our studio was on the sixth floor of one of the high-rise buildings. It had comfortable beds, a balcony and a good bathroom with endless hot water. We had to use our sheet sleeping bags and lightweight towels that we carry for the refuges. This form of accommodation is a good solution in June in Isola 2000, for the resort closes at the end of the ski season and the hotels and most of the restaurants do not open again until mid July, when they have their short summer season. At 71€ total for the studio per night it is a reasonably economical stopover for 3 or 4 people. Fortunately a fairly basic restaurant was open in the evening to serve people carrying out renovations in the resort and there was a shop where we bought food for the next day.

Day 7: Isola 2000 to Rifugio del Laus (1913m)
20.8km, ascent 1884m, descent 1900 m, 8h30
High point the Tete Rougnous 2694m

This was one of the best day's walk of our traverse of the Alps once the Col de la Lombarde had been reached. The route from there follows the Italian/French border ridge in a generally westerly direction and crosses some magnificent, but challenging terrain.

After dropping off the apartment keys in the letter box of the "agence" we followed the only footpath on the map to the east of the road that leads to the Col de la Lombarde. This path passes the permanently-closed gîte d'étape la Grange. The excoriations of ski resort machines have made route finding here difficult. Consequently it might be better to walk up the road to the Col de la Lombard and get straight to the delights that follow.

From the Col we traversed west on the Italian side of the border on a broad track that joins the border ridge and continues along this as a path for 2.5km. At this point we got our first view, on this trek, of Monte Viso that lies 50km further north at the edge of the Queyras Alps. At 3,841m this peak stands well above all its neighbours and has the unique feature of being visible from the summit of each of the peaks over 4,000m in the Alps. This is highlighted in the title of Will McLewin's book – In Monte Viso's Horizon. His account of a very individual approach to climbing all the peaks over 4000m in the Alps is a classic and a great read.

After this viewpoint the path descends on the Italian side of the border between rocks, losing some 250m before reaching the Lac di Colle di Santa Anna. At the far side of this pretty tarn we followed another twisting track that is paved with stone. This climbs back up to the border ridge at the Pas Sainte Anne, where there is a fine view south-west to the cone of Mont Mounier, a prominent peak of the Alps d'Haut Provence. The path through the col leads down to Isola, but we followed a track that winds round the head-wall of a north-facing Italian cirque to the Col de Lausfer. Halfway between the cols there is a prominent rocky spur that divides this cwm. In June 2008 most of both sections of the cwm were covered by steep snow (below), which obliterated the track. Fortunately the run-out from these snow-covered slopes was generally gentle, making the long traverse kicking steps relatively safe.

At the Col du Lausfer [65a] we disturbed some mountain goats as we started our descent to signpost [65]. There a right fork above the three frozen little Lacs Lausfer Inferieurs climbs over a low col to the larger Lac Lausfer Superieur. After passing this on its southwestern side we climbed gently to the Col de Saboule at the frontier ridge [64]. Here the path shown on the map briefly visits Italy passing some ruined fortifications. It then becomes indistinct, but some 0.8km west of the Col de Saboule we turned south back into France and then traversed below the frontier ridge. After a while we found cairns that led up a broad slope to point 2685m on the frontier ridge. This is an airy, but delightful rocky ridge (page 3) that leads to the high point of the day – the Tête Rougnouse de la Guercha.

The ridge then descends west-nor-west to point 2610m, from where there is no way forward, for the international border plunges precipitously to La Col de la Guercha. The solution is still tricky and involves descending right to a visible stony path that leads up to the Pas du Boeuf (Passo del Bue). This is a breach in a sharp rocky ridge that runs north from the frontier. After squeezing past a snow plug that was largely blocking this breach we made our way down a series of long, narrow and exposed ledges (below) to a zigzagging "path" on steep,

slippery slate scree. This eventually leads to safer ground in the Vallone della Guercia. The descent from the Pas du Boeuf would be highly problematical in snow or poor visibility. It is certainly no way for anyone lacking a head for heights. An alternative to this delicate route heads east from the approach to the Pas du Boeuf on a path that winds round to the north into the Vallone della Sauma and then leads to the road to St Bernolfo, 280m below the Rifugio del Laus. This alternative route would add about an extra hour and a half to an already-long day.

Once we had reached the Valone della Guercha from the Pas du Boeuf there was a relatively straightforward walk on snow down the valley to the Lago San Bernolfo. The ochre-painted Rifugio del Laus www.cuneo360.it/rifugi/9 lies just over the col on the west side of this lake. Accommodation on a half-board basis had been booked via the guardian's mobile phone. Normally this rifugio only opens on Saturdays and Sundays outside July and August unless a prior booking is made. Emilio Belmondo the guardian greeted us and said that he had been concerned that we might have had trouble negotiating the Pas du Boeuf. After serving us beer he left us with his heavily pregnant partner, who looked after us well.

Day 8: Rifugio del Laus to St Étienne de Tinée (1145m)
17km, ascent 776m, descent 1637m, 5h00
High point the Passo del Laroussa 2471m

This walk starts on a well made stony track heading west-south-west up the Valone di Collalunga. Soon the track became a snow plod, so we deviated left onto old moraine and picked our way through snow-free rocks and clumps of mertile (blueberry) until there was nothing but snow at the border. Just after the frontier there is a hollow with two small lakes (below), which we passed on our right before reaching the high point of the day, the Pas de Colle Longue [59a].

From the pass we headed west on the snow-free sunny side of the hill on an almost horizontal path. Rusting barbed wire was scattered on the surrounding grass. This is presumably is a remnant of border defences of the 1939-1945 war. Gradually the path moves onto a steep south-facing incline and slowly descends southwest until it reaches a gently sloping meadow at 2403m. From here we headed west for 1.5km before turning sharply east-nor-east as we crossed a ridge. The path then winds round the back of a pretty hanging valley, with a small lake at its base, before zigzagging down through steep meadows, with ever-increasing numbers of flowers, to a lane. We followed this lane northwest down to the main D2205 road in the Tinée Valley and turned right crossing the Tinée road bridge.

Almost immediately after the bridge we followed a new minor road with a green-painted cycle track that leads off to the right towards St Étienne de Tinée. This road is not shown on our IGN 1:25k map and we found it only after we had been on a wild goose chase following a lane on the other side of the river. Landslides on the north side of the Tinée have led to this lane being closed after a km or so and the bridge that used to link this to St Étienne has been demolished. The IGN map we used in 2008 needs revision. Half way to St Étienne the new road is joined by GR5, our first encounter with this trade route. The gîte d'étape le Corborant www.gite-tinee-mercantour.com/ is on the GR5 at the entrance to St Étienne de Tinée. After we had dropped off our rucksacks we walked into the old town of St Étienne with its narrow traffic-free streets. At a cafe in the square near the church we spent a happy hour or so in the warm afternoon sun watching the world go by. Both St Étienne and its gîte d'étape are worth a visit.

Day 9: St Étienne de Tinée to the Refuge de Vens (2380m)
10.8km ascent 1814m, descent 607m, 5h30
High point the Crête des Babarottes 2509m

This day's walk is a relatively short distance but it involves a steep and long assent from the Tinée valley to the Chemin de l'Énergie. This is a grassy track that runs horizontally along the northern wall of the Tinée valley at about 2300m. It was built for an ambitious hydroelectric project in the first decade of the 20th century, but the project was halted by the First World War and never restarted. The beauty of the lakes on the approach to the Refuge de Vens and the hills that surround this refuge make this a walk to savour rather than rush.

After leaving GR5 in the old town we made our way through the narrow streets to the bridge at the NW corner of St Étienne. On the far side of the bridge we turned left and after a few metres at [108] took a path to the right. This zigzags steeply up to the north gaining 600m altitude before crossing a path at [109]. There was then more zigzagging upwards until the path reached the Chemin de l'Énergie at the Mercantor Park border and signpost [112]. The chemin provides a fast route along the north side of the Tinée valley and after turning left we made good progress until a steep snow-filled gully blocked our way. We could not see the outrun from the gully, which appeared to become very steep, so a slip here could not be entertained. Fortunately with ice axes it was possible to cross this obstacle with reasonable confidence. There was a further similar snow-filled gully a little further on. Finally the chemin peters out in a boulder field. Here at [113] we took a path going just west of north that crosses the boulders and climbs to the Crête des Babarottes.

Once over this ridge the path descends to the Lac des Babarottes, which we passed to our right before making another descent to the lowest of les Lacs de Vens. We passed between this lake and the next, crossing the outflow from the latter (below) by a wooden bridge. A

profusion of brilliant sky-blue trumpet gentians covered the alp on the far side of this bridge. The path next passes to the northwest of three more lakes and then climbs a granite headland that separates the highest and largest of the lakes from its neighbours.

The Refuge de Vens lies at the head of the top lake on a rocky outcrop between two waterfalls. This is another refuge run by the Nice branch of the CAF www.cafnice.org/site/refuge/vens/. As with most CAF refuges we had made our booking and paid a deposit on line.

The wonderful location of the hut gives it a majestic view from the terrace (below). We arrived in time for a late lunch and spent a lazy afternoon reading and catching up with our logs. The weather was perfect on this midsummer's eve, making the Refuge de Vens an enchanting place to spend the solstice.

Day 10: Refuge de Vens to Larche (1666m)
22.6km, ascent 1175m, descent 1849m, 7h30
High point Pas de Morgon 2735m

It was another clear breathless morning, which helped route finding during the parts of this long day where we crossed trackless high hills. From the refuge we headed north, still in the shadow of the frontier ridge to our right. The path led us in long zigzags to the Collet de Tortisse [35a] and sunshine. Southwest along the ridge from this col are bizarrely shaped rock outcrops – the Aiguilles de Tortisse. Our way headed in the opposite direction to the Col de Fer and the Italian border. This involved crossing some extraordinarily slippery, but happily not steep, snow patches. The base of these patches was hard ice, while the melt induced by the early morning sun alarmingly lubricated the surface under our trainers. At the col there was a fine view into Italy with the unmistakable split cone of Monte Viso again visible in the background.

At the Col de Fer we left marked paths and headed north and then north-west up the frontier ridge to the Pas de Morgan. The route was along an interesting and varied crest. Despite considerable snow the ridge presented no difficulties apart from a short climb up steep snow on the final approach to the pass. The route onwards is shown below and is truly trackless. Our goal the Pas de Cavale can be pinpointed above the place where grass continues almost 2/3rds of the way up the steep scree on the far side of the valley.

From the Pas de Morgon we went to the right of the part-snow-covered knoll in the foreground of the picture. After rounding this we headed just north of west on the left side of a stream. This led across increasingly grassy slopes, which in places were steep, but not difficult as we could pick the line of least resistance. After crossing the main valley stream we climbed to [37] where we once more joined GR5.

Our trackless walk from the Pas de Morgon had not been difficult and it is hard to understand why there is no path on this route. Fortunately, the weather had been perfect, but if it had been misty navigation might have posed some problems. We returned to a path on rejoining GR5 near the point where the way to the Col de Pauriac forks to the right. The red and white way-marks of GR5 led us upwards in zigzags passing above and to the left of the 3 small Lacs de Agnel. As we got higher the grassy buttress petered out. The way ahead now crossed steep scree and this led to a rock wall that looked challenging. Somehow a way opened up and the final ascent to the Pas de Cavale was spectacular, but in no way difficult.

The views from the Pas de la Cavale in all directions were very fine and we lingered there for some time before beginning the long descent down the Vallon du Lauzanier. At first we traversed large snow slopes (below) on the way to the upper lake - the Lac de Derrière la Croiz. Ahead of us in the distance lay the Chambeyron hills, which we were to walk through the following day. Further down the snow gave way to green alp as we continued to the Lac du Lauzanier. While passing this lake we started to meet groups of people walking up from the road-head. After the lake the path descends to a less scenic lower valley, known as Val Fouran. In the flat bottom of this valley the path becomes a track that 2.5km further on passes into a car park.

GR5 exits to the left from the car park on a poorly-maintained lane that gradually winds round to the northwest following the left flank of the valley of the Ubayette for 3.5km. The road and GR5 then cross the river Ubayette and join the main road from the Col de Larch and Italy. One km down this road we entered the small village of Larche (opposite seen the following day from the north)

We had booked accommodation at the excellent gîte d'étape Grand Traverse des Alps www.gite-etape-larche.com/. This is on the left at the entrance to the village. The wall of the gîte facing the road and the side walls are metal clad and painted grey. By contrast the southern side, which faces the river has a pleasant wooden facade fronted by a lawn with tables, where we enjoyed our usual post-walk beer. The food at the gîte was superb, the welcome great, the showers hot, the bunks comfortable and the value exceptional. It was the name of this gîte and possibly the beer they served that first induced in us the concept of undertaking an extended walk across the Alps from the Mediterranean to the Adriatic Sea.

Day 11: Larche to Fouillouse (1872m)
18.4km, ascent 1639m, descent 1444m, 7h15
High point the Pas de la Couletta 2752m

The route from Larch starts on the GR5, zigzagging up the open alp north of the village and gaining almost 1,000m before reaching the Col de Mallemort at 2558m. Just over this col the path passes to the right of les Baraquements de Viraysse. These ruined barracks date from 1882 and lie at the south end of a fine high valley surrounded by a series of rocky pointed peaks. On the far side of the ruins we gradually descended northwest to a stream before climbing to the Col du Vallonet. The path then forks and GR5 takes the line of least resistance to the left. We headed right past the north side of the Lac du Vallonnet Superieur. From there the path winds counter clockwise round a knoll - the Tête de Plate Lombarde. At the north-eastern end of this knoll, where the path forks again, we turned left and continued to the northwest for a further 1.4 km. We then turned right and climbed just north of east up a beautiful alp to the highest point on the Menton to

Briançon leg of our walk, the Pas de la Couletta (below). The rock peak of the Brec de Chambeyron towers above the eastern flank of the pass, while the elegant Aiguille de Chambeyron, the highest peak of this range of hills, rises from the other side of the high valley ahead. Just after the pass we took a left fork, descending steeply northwest on a slate scree path past the east side of the Lac Premier to the open, but at that time unmanned, Refuge de Chambeyron. Our path then traverses under the Bec de Roux descending westwards to Fouillouse.

In this pretty village, with shingle-roofed houses, we stayed at the Gîte les Granges www.gitelesgranges.com/en/. This gîte is located on the right at the lower end of the sloping cobbled street. Its dining room, where we had an excellent meal, is in the vaulted cellar of this large old stone house. We slept in a small dortoir with beds rather than bunks and there were very welcome hot showers. Despite this being a Monday night in June the gîte was full, so we had been wise to book.

Day 12: Fouillouse to Refuge de Basse Rua (1750m)
15.8km, ascent 1342m, descent 1454m, 6h15
High point the Col de Serenne 2674m

The following morning we left Fouillouse, again starting on the GR5. This heads right from the road at the bottom of the village. The path traverses for a while before climbing round the lip of a cirque. It then enters woods and descends to the road that links Fouillouse with the

Ubaye valley. We followed this road down to the spectacular Pont du Châtelet, which spans the high vertical rock walls of the gorge of the Ubaye river (below).

Some 200m beyond the bridge the road joins the D25, where we turned right. It appears that the current trade route into the Queyras Alps via the Col de Serenne leaves the road shortly after crossing a bridge that spans the torrent draining the Vallon de Serenne. This path follows the torrent on its northeast side. Unfortunately we had selected to take an un-classified route marked on the IGN 1:25k map that ascends on the southwest side of the torrent. This route is no longer serviceable, has no waymarks and is not signposted from the road. In several places it is overgrown. After passing the abandoned houses of the summer hill hamlet of Haut Coulet the "path" traverses steep unstable hillside uncomfortably high above the torrent. In places the path has slipped away and progress along this route was difficult and dangerous. This relic of a path should be avoided. Eventually the gorge

ends, opening into the broad grassy Serenne valley. At this point there is a shack built against a boulder, which is marked on the map with the grandiose title - Cabane Sous le Rocher. After this shelter a path waymarked with orange flashes runs on the right side of the valley stream leading to the Col de Serenne.

From the col the path continues down the long, wide and grassy Vallon Laugier. There are great views of the distant snow-capped eastern peaks of the Ecrins both from the col and on the descent. After passing a bergerie to our right we followed the path across the stream to the end of the hanging Laugier valley. There is then a steep descent through woods to the floor of the main Escreins Valley where the path passes over the dry stone beds to the left of the river. On reaching a track we followed this across the river to the Refuge de Basse Rua www.refuge-basserua.fr/. This modern refuge, run by Eric Disdier, is delightfully situated. It offers everything the walker could want. We were the only guests and after a fine meal we watched the sun set over the Écrins (below). At dusk our host told us he was going down to Guilestre to be with his wife, but he returned early the next morning to provide our breakfast.

Day 13: Refuge de Basse Rua to Ceillac (1636m)
15.8km, ascent 1778m, descent 1890m, 7h00
High point the Pic d'Escreins 2734m

This is a wonderful day of challenging walking across the jagged peaks that separate the Escreins and Ceillac valleys. The route is on GR58, which starts from the refuge de Basse Rua and provides an interesting and airy route up the cliffs to the north of the refuge. There are some metal steps and fixed ropes to protect in tricky places. On reaching the top of the cliff there is a long traverse to the west, to a point where a broad path climbs in long zigzags to a col just below and to the north of the summit of the Pic d'Escreins. It is then a short walk to this summit, which is a magnificent view point.

After returning to the col we followed the GR, which descends eastwards into a large stony bowl. From the base of this hollow the path turns north and climbs onto the Crête d'Andreveysson. This ridge is grassy at the start, but then becomes an airy white grit buttress (below), which we walked down before entering a steep gully that provides a safe means to descend the cliffs to the right of the crête and reach the Vallon des Pelouses.

This vallon was indeed covered with lush green grass and the route here is marked by short wooden posts with red and white bands on the top. These lead past the south side of the Bergerie Andrevez and into a horizontal grassy lateral-valley, where there is a waymark on some slabs to the left of the path. From the exit of the valley the GR58 apparently climbs up to the right gaining some 120m before contouring on the steep wall of the Créte de la Mourière. Unfortunately we were seduced by a well-trodden path that descends from the end of the lateral valley and then traverses right before petering out in a steep trackless cwm with scrub-covered walls. It involved some free scrambling up this cwm to return to GR58. We then traversed on the waymarked path round the crest of the crête to the Belvedere de la Mourière from where we could look down to Ceillac 600m below. The remainder of the walk descends on a good stony path, still waymarked with red and white flashes, to this large village.

At the southern edge of old Ceillac we found the gîte d'étape Les Baladins www.baladins.queyras.com. It is yet another excellent lodging house. Again the food is good and we were given a room with 4-double-tier bunks plus a shower, toilet and balcony, which we shared with 2 other walkers. After a shower we enjoyed wandering round the centre of Ceillac village, which has several picturesque antique wooden buildings and a fine wooden fountain with the vertical planks retaining the water that are bound together by metal hoops.

Day 14: Ceillac to La Chalp d'Arvieux (1678m)
20.1km, ascent 1589m, descent 1622m, 7h30
High point the Col Fromage 2301m

The route on the last two days to Briançon faithfully follows GR5 and is predictably relatively easy going, but of continued interest. We left Ceillac on a lane heading northeast and soon followed a path diagonally up the hillside to the left. After passing the Chapel Ste. Barbe there is a division of paths and GR5 continues NE climbing on a well-graded and partially-shaded path to the Col Fromage. From the col the path heads northwards contouring below the Crête de la Selle and then through the edge of forestry. Some 2.5km from the col the path crosses a broad ridge and then descends in zigzags into a valley and continues gently down this valley to Château Queyras (below). The GR flashes assist route finding through the flowered pastures where in places numerous cattle tracks make it difficult otherwise to identify the correct way. The château is an impressive fortification sited on top of a rocky outcrop that rises on the north side of the River Guil.

GR5 crosses the river on a road bridge and then climbs up through the village to the main road, which we followed westwards. After passing the château we continued through one loop and then headed north from the road climbing steeply in zizags through pine woods.

Eventually the path arrives at the south end of the Lac de Roue, a good place on a hot day for a rest in the shade of surrounding trees. From the lake we descended through exquisite fields filled with wild flowers to les Maisons. We skirted to the east side of this hamlet and then traversed northwards through woods above the village of Arvieux and on to la Chalp and the gîte d'étape/chambre d'hôte - le Chalet Viso www.chaletviso.com. This spacious gîte is another excellent stopover.

Day 15: La Chalp d'Arvieux to Briançon (1205m)
19.1km, ascent 978m, descent 1440m, 6h15
High point the Col des Ayes 2477m

On this last day of the walk to Briançon we went from la Chalp along the road towards the Col d'Izoard. After a few minutes and just before the village of Brunissard, we turned left onto a lane that skirts the village and followed this for 3 km to a car park. From there GR5 continues on a track that goes through 3 bends before reaching a large flat grassy area – la Pré Premier. This is surrounded by hills and has a lake at its far end. Here GR5 was not well waymarked, but it continues up a track that climbs from the right side of the meadow. After this track rounds the southwest ridge of a hill it flattens off in alpine meadows. Now a signpost indicates GR5 leading to the right up grassy slopes to the Col des Ayes (below), the last high pass before Briançon.

The descent was through beautiful sun-drenched floral meadows passing the two Chalets de Vers le Col on our way to the Chalets des Ayes. Just before this village there was another delightful meadow (below). The lane running through the village continues along the base of the valley, splitting about a km after the last house. We took the higher left fork on a track that traverses through forest still towards the nor-nor-west. Where the track winds round to the west GR5 descends northwards on a path to a lane that zigzags down to Sachas.

From this village we abandoned GR5 and continued northwards on the road towards Briançon, passing the station. From there it is a further 2.2km walk with 147m ascent to the old walled city with its attractive narrow streets. The Hotel Cristol www.hotel-cristol-briancon.fr/ is situated on the road circling the north side of the old city. It is good value, comfortable Logis Hotel and convenient if one is continuing the walk, for it is close to the start of the next leg. If the walk is broken at Briançon there is a choice of hotels near the station. From there regular trains run to Lyon, Aix en Provence and Marseille where there are TGV connections and links to Lyon and Marseille Airports.

2 CHAPTER
BRIANÇON-ST GINGOLPH
The second half of the walk from the Mediterranean to Lake Geneva

Day 16: Briançon to Névache Ville Haute (1620m)
20.4km, ascent 1711m, descent 1443m, 7h45
High point la Grande Peyrolle 2587m

The walk to Névache begins by climbing steeply from the north side of the old city of Briançon gaining 1150m to reach the Serre des Aigles. My grandsons tell me that it is best to use a via ferrata to scale the first 600m of this climb and reach the top of the cliff that provides the backdrop to the main street of the old city. We decided to follow the more restrained route provided by GR5c. It starts by a fountain 0.2km west of the Hotel Cristol on a lane that rises from the Route d'Italie. This lane runs north-eastwards below the cliff to the Fort des Sallettes. From there a well-graded path zigzags up steep wooded hillside on the eastern flank of the cliff to the Croix de Toulouse. This notable belvedere is the top of the via ferrata, but we were still only halfway to the Serre des Aigles and there was better to come. At first after the Croix de Toulouse the climb is relatively gentle on a path that makes long zigzags through woods west of the Crête de Malefosse. The path then joins this crête at a col with an ancient military building. After this there is a steep, but enjoyable climb up rocks to the 2567m summit. This scramble is clearly waymarked and relatively straightforward. Despite the impressive height gain we were still only 3km as the crow flies from the city walls.

Days 16-30 Briançon to St Gingolph

From the summit we could see the high Écrins to the south-west (above), while in the opposite direction was the string of border hills. Far below lay Briançon with the Durance Valley stretching away to the south. Our way ahead was northwards along a sharp airy ridge (below). Half way along the ridge the path briefly contours below the summits

39

of the Petite and then the Grande Peyrolles, but the following 2km are again on the crest of the ridge. This crosses the quartz Croix de la Chime and two further tops. There is then a skidding descent northwestwards on steep loose quartz gravel to the Col de Barteaux. The ridge we had just walked along had been of continued interest. In places it had threatened to have tricky exposed sections, but in the good conditions we had enjoyed it delighted without causing problems.

After the Col de Barteaux our path headed west across a high plateau on its way to a road-head at the Col de Granon (2404m). On the far side of the road we passed a chalet and joined a track heading west-nor-west. Some 1.75 km along this track we turned left at a fork and continued with little additional ascent to the Port de Cristol.

There was no wind by this time and we had the hill to ourselves as we made our way down past the small Lac Rood and then the larger Lac de Cristol (above). Shortly after descending through the tree line we reached a clearing where the path divides. The GR5c, goes to the right without crossing the stream, but to continue on this would make a long detour to the east of our destination via la Ville Bas de Névache. We followed a more direct route that turns left across a bridge over the Cristol Stream. This good path was signposted as going towards the Chalets de Buffère, but almost immediately after the bridge we turned right onto a less than distinct and non-waymarked path that is shown heading north on the 1:25k IGN map. At first this crosses marshy ground, but soon the path becomes clearer and there was no difficulty following it down steep zigzags through forest to the west of the Cristol stream. The path levels off as it enters the main Névache valley and approaches the river Clarée. Now the way again becomes less distinct. Undeterred, we continue north through the scrub as best we could until we reached GR57, which runs along the south bank of the river. Heading right on this good path we soon reached a bridge that leads into to the attractive Haute Ville de Névache.

We continued through this small, largely traffic-free, ancient village and a few yards beyond the church took a track to the left. This leads to the gîte d'étape le Creux des Souches, where we were to stay the night http://lecreuxdessouches.com/. Unfortunately, while we were on our long and strenuous walk, a group of youngsters had arrived by bus and installed themselves on the bottom and second tier bunks in the dortoir. Consequently we were privileged to enjoy the top level of the unusual three-tiered bunks. It proved quite an adventure to leave and return to these births in the dark, an occasional requirement of male walkers *d'un certain age*. Future mature visitors might consider booking a room rather than space in this dortoir. We had been given that option when booking these lodgings, but unfortunately had chosen the bunk room. Apart from this inconvenience the welcome, hot showers, food and other facilities at le Creux des Souches were all excellent.

Day 17: Névache Haute Ville to Ref du Mont Thabor (2502m)
17.1km, ascent 1624m, descent 691m, 6h30
High point the Refuge du Mt Thabor 2502m

We left the gîte going east through the Haute Ville to the valley road and soon passed through the Ville Basse de Névache. Some 0.3km beyond this we veered diagonally left onto a side road that passes through la Chapelle des Ammes. Near the end of this village the road divides and we took the left fork that continues eastwards, almost immediately joining GR5. This takes a more easterly route than GR5c from Briançon to this point. We turned left again onto a stony track that winds across fields towards the narrow entrance to the Roubion valley. The track then passes through forest along the west bank of the Roubion stream. After a while it crosses a bridge over a tributary and enters a small glade with a shaded picnic table and a foresters' cabin. From there we followed the red and white waymarks of the GR on a path above and to the left of the stream. Eventually the path converges with and crosses this stream. It then winds up the forested steep right side of the valley circling round the back of an immense natural obelisk. The path finally emerges from the forest onto the green pasture of the shallow Vallon de Thorse. At the north end of this meadow at the Col de Thorse (2194m) there was a fine view over the small Lac Cavillon to the snowy slopes of Mont Thabor (below).

Passing to the east of the lake we descended on a good path that winds down the steep southern wall of the Vallée Etroite. Although this valley is still France it drains to the river Po and was Italian until the post Second World War peace treaty signed in Paris in 1947. Near the base of the valley lay the Refuge Tre Alpini surrounded by meadows with white St Bruno Lilies bobbing their delicate heads in the breeze.

It was too early for lunch at the refuge, so we continued north-west up the left side of the lightly-wooded floor of the Valleé Étroite. The track comes to an end as it reaches a prominent waterfall in the headwall of the lower valley. Two paths climb from the base of the falls. The left path leads to Mont Thabor, but we followed GR5 to the right and north across the Pont de la Fonderie. This ascends past rocks to the upper valley. The route continues on this path to the watershed at the Col de la Vallée Etroite. Here we passed a wooden cross and followed a path that winds round a pond before undulating westwards to the Refuge du Mont Thabor: http://refugeduthabor.com/. The sleeping quarters in series of small bunk rooms are comfortable. By contrast the washing and toilet facilities are at best parsimonious. Maybe a dip in the icy waters of the adjacent Lac Ste Marguerite would be a good solution later in the season. This lake is reached by a walk of a minute or two over a low ridge to the west of the hut. There was a stunning view (below) from the shore of the lake across snow-patched hillside to the rocky peak of the Cheval Blanc (3020m), which lies just to the north of Mont Thabor.

Day 18: Ref Mont Thabor to Aussois (1488m)
26.1km, ascent 1700m, descent 2737m, 9h30 or
20.3km, ascent 755m, descent 1781m, 6h15
High point for both routes the Ref du Mt Thabor 2502m

The walk down from the Refuge leads to the Arc Valley and the railway town of Modane. From there we climbed into the Vanoise Alps, which we were to cross during the next 5 days.

On leaving the refuge we contoured northwards across snow on the headwall of a broad cirque. The path soon emerged from beneath the snow and curved round to the north-east following the left side of the valley stream. Eventually after passing some buildings to our left the path crossed the stream and we rejoined GR5. This becomes a track that descends steeply through 4 zigzags before the incline eases and the track becomes a road that passes a small dammed lake. Some 0.25km past the dam the GR leaves the road, crosses the outflow stream and descends through woods to the Hamlet of les Herbiers. Here we crossed back over the stream and continued to Charmaix. At the far end of this village the GR turns left from the road onto a track that leads to Notre Dame du Charmaix. This chapel is set in a cliff high above a torrent. We followed the pilgrim route from the chapel to Modane, passing a series of shrines along its length. Lower down the route rejoins and follows the road through two hairpins before continuing once again as a path heading north-east to an underpass beneath the main road to the Frejus road tunnel. A little later the path reaches the south side of the railway and follows this to the entrance of the rail tunnel to Italy. Here it crosses the railway on a bridge incorporated into the arch of the tunnel entrance. It then doubles back to lanes that lead gently down into Modane. After lunch at a café in the main square we crossed a road bridge over the rapidly-flowing and

substantial river Arc. On the far side the short route to Aussois turns right onto the D215 road, which leads in around 7km to this attractive small mountain town.

It is a much tougher day to take the longer and more scenic route from Modane to Aussois. This alternative continues north from the bridge to the edge of the town and then climbs steadily on a path through trees. At a fork the route goes to the right on GR5 (the left fork is GR 55). GR5 then zigzags up though the woods in a northerly direction until at 1,900m it starts to traverse, passing first below the Refuge de l'Orgère and then above the Refuge de l'Aiguille Doran. Gradually it climbs to a high point at the Col du Barbier, where there is a fine view across a lake, with a large barrage, to the 3639m Dent Parrachée (above). To reach Aussois we left GR5 here and took a steep path diagonally down to the west end of the barrage. On reaching the lake we turned right past the dam and followed a path that descends to an unclassified lane. Along the lane to the left we went through a right-hand bend before taking a path that leads down across a grassy ski run to the base of the Aussois ski lifts. Our hotel - Les Mottets www.hotel-lesmottets.com/ lies on a road to the west off the top of the main street in Aussois. This is a pleasant and comfortable logis hotel where JS and I had stayed on our tour of the Vanoise in 2006. It was well worth the return visit

Day 19: Aussois to Refuge de l'Arpont (2309m)
18.7km, ascent 1953m, descent 1152m, 7h30
High point the Roc des Corneilles 2466m

There is a long, pleasant and generally gentle ascent from Aussois back to the GR5, which stays high and contours above the back of the barraged lake that we passed towards the end of the previous day. Our route starts at the top of the village by the base of the ski lifts on the road that winds up to the barrage. Before the first bend we followed a path that takes a more direct line to 1780m where it rejoins the road. Almost immediately we took a right fork from the road onto a track heading north. This meanders up pleasant wooded hillside until just above 1900m where it meets the boundary of the Vanoise national park. The boundary is marked with horizontal red white and blue tricolour bands. After a south-pointing hairpin bend the track curves round to the west and we took a path to the right that heads up the hill through woods to the northeast. This path steepens as it crosses a rock-band and once past this there is a further stiff climb through meadows to the grassy Col la Turra at 2363m and the junction with GR5. A signpost here indicates that it is a further 4h30 walk to our destination.

GR5 climbs from the col to a track that contours at around 2460m, allowing fast progress across the steep grassy hillside high above the Arc valley and beneath the Dent Parrachée. The route passes above ruins at la Loza and then as a path turns north-east entering a large scree-filled cirque. After crossing a stream we climbed across the large scree slope to a high point at 2471m. There is then a descent of some 300m to a ruin marked Montafia on the map. From there the path climbs once more into another cirque before descending first to a boiling torrent and then to the abandoned hamlet at le Mont. After this a steady climb northwards leads eventually to the Refuge l'Arpont. This

CAF refuge www.arpont.refuges-vanoise.com/ has 3 stone buildings. It was busy, but the guardian coped well. We received a good welcome and the food was satisfying. Our accommodation was in a large functional dortoir with 2-tiered multi-birth bunks. Since then the refuge has been closed for refurbishment, but it reopened in June 2014.

Day 20: Refuge de l'Arpont to Refuge de la Leisse (2489m)
17.3km, ascent 1215m, descent 1057m, 6h00
High point the East flank of Chasseforêt, 2581m

The route stays above 2000m for the whole of this day's delectable walk. The first section continues along GR5 high on the west flank of the quiet and substantial side valley from the Arc that heads north from Termignon. In the first km or so the path climbs 350m to a high point from where we could see the distinctive snow-capped dome of the Grande Motte (3653) to the north. The protection of wildlife in the Vanoise national park has led to remarkably tame flocks of Ibex (above). The French, German and Italian names for these magnificent creatures are respectively Bouquetin, Steinbock and Stambecco. They are frequently seen along this section of GR5.

From the day's high-point the route levels off, contouring through four varied and interesting cirques below the massive ice field formed by the glaciers of the high plateau of the Dôme de l'Arpont. After the last cirque the path winds between small lakes under the red rock face of Mont Pelve. This was a good place to eat our picnic (below).

From the lakes the path turns to the east and climbs gently before descending in zigzags to a farm west of the confluence of the Leisse and Rocheure torrents. The GR crosses these rivers by two adjacent bridges and then continues on a stony track on the south bank of the Rocheure. At a further bridge GR5 heads south, but our way was north on GR55 across the bridge. This follows a track that climbs past the Refuge d'Entre Deux Eaux and the Chapelle St-Pierre. It continues on to the east bank of the Leisse, passing an old stone bridge that carries a

path leading up to the Col de la Vanoise. We stayed on the eastern bank of the river and headed up the Vallon de la Leisse. Long stretches of this section of the Leisse were still covered with snow. Much of this appeared to have avalanched from the steep scree and rocky hillside that rises on the far side of the river to the ridge between the Grande Motte and the Grande Casse, which at 3852m is the highest point in the Vanoise. By contrast, it was a gentle and pleasant climb up the south side of the valley.

Thunder sounded as the refuge came into view, loftily perched on a rocky bluff on the far side of the river. Although the pace quickened it started to rain and as there was still a good half hour to go we were obliged to put on our waterproofs. After crossing the river there was a

50m climb round the back of the bluff up to the 3 wooden buildings that make up the refuge de la Leisse http://refugedelaleisse.e-monsite.com/. The guardienne provided a warm welcome and we were able to dry out by her stove. The refuge has 32 places in multi-birth bunks. Toilets were in a shed a short way down the hill and washing facilities at a wooden trough set in the middle of a grassy patch with a fine view down the valley. Splashing away at this trough the following morning with hens pecking about on the surrounding grass had a certain appeal. Those contemplating a stop at this delightful refuge may be pleased to read the proud new comment on their website – *"Il y a une douche et Chaude en plus!!!!"*

Day 21: *Refuge de la Leisse to Refuge Entre le Lac (2146m)*
18.2km, ascent 1020m, descent 1316m, 6h00
High point the Col de la Leisse 2761m

This high-level excursion climbs to the Col de la Leisse (2761m), the highest point on the walk between Menton and Lake Geneva. A 600m descent to Val Claret follows before a climb to the Col du Palet (2673m) and descent to the refuge Entre le Lac.

We set off from our stopover climbing to a dam, where the path goes clockwise round a large lake. Although it was overcast there was light in the sky and the absence of wind enabled spectacular zebra-like reflections of the snow-patched hills (below). The path continues past the five Lacs de la Leisse with the snow underfoot becoming continuous as we approached the Col. Our view west from the top of the pass looked up to the summer ski slopes of the Grande Motte where skiers, who were no more than moving dots, wound down the distant glacier. The descent from the col heads north-east for 2km before joining the boundary of the Vanoise Park and curving round to the west-nor-west. Here the path comes to a ski lift where we took a left fork onto a minor path that heads steeply down into a grassy valley away from GR55. At the end of the valley we reached a semicircular road that skirts the southern end of the Val Claret ski station.

It is a steep climb north-west from the SW corner of the resort, passing under the cables of 3 ski lifts before meeting up once again with the GR5. This GR goes over the col de l'Iseran near the only road across the Vanoise, some considerable way east of the route we had taken. On joining GR5 we headed southwest and then west, climbing to the Col du Palet (below). The descent from this col re-enters the Vanoise Park passing to the south of the Refuge du Col du Palet and continuing to the west end of the Lac du Grattaleau. Shortly after passing the Chalet de la Grassaz we turned left from GR5 onto a path

that contours below the Aiguille de Bacque and 200m above the Lac de la Plagne. The Refuge Entre le Lac is visible from here at the southwest end of the lake. Rather than sticking to the path, which contours round the cirque before descending, we scrambled down the grassy hillside to the lake and on to our lodging. This beautifully sited refuge is privately-owned and well worth a visit http://refuge-entre-le-lac-vanoise.over-blog.com/. It has a large comfortable dortoir with well-spaced two-tier single bunks. Hot showers are available and the food is good.

Day 22: Refuge Entre le Lac to Valezan (1174m)
21.0km, ascent 1159m, descent 2104m, 7h15
High point the Refuge Entre le Lac 2167m

The walk to Valezan passes the last of the high mountains of the Vanoise range, crosses the River Isère and then climbs into the Beaufort Alps. From the refuge the path heads north passing to the west of the Lac de la Plagne and the stream that flows out of the lake. The floor of this section of the beautiful valley is known as the Plan des Eaux and as the name implies is an almost flat water meadow. At this hour it was still in shade, while the great rock-faces that rise steeply on either side were already lit by the morning sun (below). We rejoined GR5 as it starts a 900m steep descent to a lower valley on a path that loops down the left side of a cliff. The natural luxuriant rock gardens on this descent were a delight and we lingered to savour the varied masses of early summer flowers. After reaching the road-head at the Chalet-Refuge de Rosuel we turned right from the road after a few metres and crossed the river. A track on the far bank led to a to the hamlet of Beaupraz, where we crossed the river again and stopped at a chalet for some coffee. This was served at a table on the lawn by a water trough where we enjoyed the warm sunshine and wonderful surroundings (below).

GR5 continues in woods on the far side of the main valley road passing old mine works at les Lanches. This pleasant shaded track continues on the south side of the river to a bridge that leads to the village of le Moulin. Here GR5 crosses the bridge, but we chose to follow a more challenging variant on the south side of the river. This continues on the track for three or four hundred metres before following a path that climbs steeply through the woods on the left side of the valley. At times this path is quite exposed, but never becomes desperate. Eventually the path starts to descend and the woods begin to thin. We then walked down the edge of a steep grassy ski slope before entering the attractively-renovated and expanded village of Montchavin, where we managed to find a bar for a light lunch.

From Montchavin we headed west through fields to Montorlin before descending on a largely shaded path to a bridge over the River Isère. We crossed both the river and the N90 road to get to Bellentre, from where we climbed on a broad path to the west-nor-west that led to the village of Valezan. This was a long hot haul, but there was welcome shade on much of the route. The popular l'Auberge Valezan www.gite-auberge-valezan.com/ lies near the top of the village and has fine views back to the Vanoise hills. This stop is very comfortable with great washing facilities, single bunks and good food. My son Andrew joined us again at this stage. He had flown to Lyon where he took a train to the station at Aime la Plagne. This lies 6km west of the Auberge Valezan and there is a 600m ascent along the D86 from the station to the auberge.

Day 23: Valezan to Refuge du Plan de la Lai (1818m)
19.7km, ascent 1767m, descent 1170m, 7h30
High point the Col du Bresson 2469m

This walk follows GR 5 all day through the Beaufort Alps. To the left along the road from the gîte lies the centre of the old village of Valezan. Here the GR heads left uphill past old houses and shops. At the top of the village the road becomes a track that climbs northwest up open hillside on the south side of the Isère Valley. The track joins a lane at la Lance and after this hamlet we turned right onto a path that follows the line of a dry aqueduct through rich hay fields. The grass emitted clouds of pollen as we pushed through its long stems gradually contouring round to the north and entering a broad valley that perfectly epitomises the terroir of Beaufort cheese. (opposite) After passing a dairy where they were making, but not maturing, cheese the path meets a stony track. This heads up the valley and then curves round to the left rising through the 2000m contour, where we came to the communal refuge at la Balme. We stopped there for a much-needed drink, for it was a warm day even at this altitude. From the hut we followed the waymarked path to the Col du Bresson (2469m), where there were fine views of the surrounding sharp rocky peaks.

There is a long descent on the west side of the col as the path gradually works its way round to the northwest, reaching a track at 1921m. We followed this to the right briefly and passed a waterfall (below) before descending on a steep shrub-lined path. This crosses the track once again before flattening out at 1770m and traversing through flower-filled meadows to cowsheds at Lavachey.

The GR5 now climbs northwards below the Aiguille du Grand Fond and high above the hydro Lac de Roselend. Springs made the path muddy where it passes through alder scrub. After reaching a col at 2050m with the ruins of la Grande Berge there was a descent through alpenrose to a stream before we climbed once more to the renovated, but locked, Petite Berge. The final descent over 3 km leads to a country road and the refuge du Plan de la Lai. The road here is frequented by masochistic cyclists toiling their way to the col at the Cormet de Roselend. We were looked after well and had a comfortable stay at this refuge http://caf.albertville.free.fr/php/spip.php?article18.

Day 24: Refuge Plan de la Lai to Hôtel-de Tré-la-Tête (1970m)
17km, ascent 1429m, descent 1291m, 6h30
High point the Crête de Grittes 2538m

In the morning we completed our traverse of the Beaufort Alps and ended the day at a quaint period chalet Hôtel-Refuge on the southwest flank of Mt Blanc.

At the start we followed GR5 climbing northeast through cow pastures, crossing a stream where milk churns, stored overnight in the cool water, were being collected. At the Col de la Sauce, we got our first view on this walk of Mt Blanc. The path from the col follows the airy ridge of the Crête des Gittes, with a high point of 2538m. Although the drops from this fine ridge are spectacular the path is always well made and secure. At the end of the ridge we descended to the Refuge du Col de la Croix du Bonhomme, were GR5 converges with the Tour du Mont Blanc. As might be expected the route now becomes more crowded. From the refuge we traversed to the Col du Bonhomme (shown opposite with the Aiguille de Bionnassay and the Dôme du Gouter in the background) and then made the long descent to the mountain restaurant at la Balme. This was a good stop for lunch, with wonderful omelettes and large mugs of refreshing beer.

After lunch we followed a stony track until a little before the village of Nant Borant, where the track enters woods. Here we left GR5 and took an unclassified path to the right dropping to and crossing a stream before turning left onto a path that goes through woods to the hamlet of la Laya. We had lost the crowds and continued to a bridge below the Cascade de Combe Noire. On the far side of this bridge there followed a long steep and tiring climb on a path that zigzaggs up through the woods. Some 400m higher we at last reached the alp where the Tré-la-Tête hotel-refuge is located www.trelatete.com/. This quaint early twentieth century establishment is well worth a visit. We were allocated a twin and a triple room both with brass bedsteads sheets and a duvet. We were not used to such comfort.

Day 25: Hôtel-de Tré-la-Tête to Hôtel-Ref. du Prarion (1853m)
19km, ascent 1741m, descent 1843m, 7h30
High point the Col de Tricot 2120m

We started this walk on a path that traverses just west of north from the hut and is marked as the "Chemin de Claudius Bernard" on the map. Surprisingly, someone had cut the grass on this path preventing our legs getting soaked by the morning dew. This beautiful and tranquil route circles round the Combe d'Armancette, before descending west through the woods to the 1400m contour. Here, above the town of les Contamines Montjoie, the path joins a track that heads north. After descending another 50m or so it heads north-east up through the forest to the alpine meadows around les Chalets du Truc. There is then a 200m descent to les Chalets de Miage. This is a good place to take on fluid before the long unshaded haul in the noon heat up 560m to the Col de Tricot. In the event the climb was less of an ordeal than we had anticipated, for the incline, though steep, is steady and the path well made.

The descent from the col was a delight, walking across alpenrose-clad hillside (below). The snow-covered peaks of the Mt Blanc Massif towered above us to our right silhouetted against the dark blue sky. We crossed the torrent flowing from the snout of the Bionnassay Glacier by an interestingly mobile wire bridge and then climbed on its far side through woods to the Chalet de l'Are. From there the route heads north-west on an airy path that traverses steep flowered hillside while gradually climbing to the broad ridge that supports the Tramway du Mt Blanc. We walked beside the tramway to the arrête at the Col de Voza, from where a broad dusty 4x4 track leads up to the Hôtel du Prarion www.prarion.com/en/index.html. This wonderfully-sited hotel sits at 1860m on the east end of the summit ridge of the Prarion. There are unrivalled views of the northern and western aspects of the Mont Blanc massive from this ridge. We had booked bunks in the dormitory, but when we arrived we were offered an upgrade to twin rooms with all comforts. It took no persuading for us to accept this offer. So we had a second night between sheets and this time with *en suite* bathrooms. The excellent evening meal was enhanced by a memorable view through the picture windows of Mt Blanc in the setting sun and the hills to the north where we were going the following day (above).

Day 26: Le Parion to Ref d'Anterne Alf. Wills (1820m)
20.6km, ascent 1799m, descent 1843m, 8h00
High point the Col d'Anterne 2257m

From the Prarion north to Lake Geneva the hillsides are again much quieter. We set off on the short walk to the summit of the Prarion, which lies just north of the hotel. It was a brilliant day and a few minutes were spent taking in the view of the Mt Blanc Massive in the still cool morning brilliance. Although the Prarion is a mere pimple compared with its lofty neighbours the descent of its northwest ridge is a highlight of the walk. It is steep and in places exposed. While it is never really dangerous there is continued interest and the prospects are magnificent. The ridge falls nearly 500m to the Col de Forclaz from where a track and then a path marked with red and yellow flashes lead northwards through beech woods. This rather neglected path becomes something of an obstacle course as it crosses over the top of the Tunnel du Châtelard, which conveniently covers the motorway going to the Mont Blanc tunnel. This green crossing leads to a lane that passes over the River Arve and enters Vieux Servoz.

From this quiet, attractive village we took a route ostentatiously named "GR de Pays Tour du Pays du Mont Blanc variante" northwards out of the village. This path climbs through beech forest and occasional fields from where there are wonderful views of the north face of Mont Blanc (below). After passing the restaurant near the Lac Vert we continued on an undulating track to the gîte d'étape at le Châtelet. This was a good place for lunch in the garden.

Next the route goes uphill on a path from the west side of the gîte that leads to a road at Ayères des Rocs where we turned right and continued through Ayères des Pierrières. Some way after this hamlet we followed a 4x4 track that heads uphill towards the Refuge de Moëde Anterne. At 1979m on the map and before the refuge we rejoined GR5 which comes from the opposite direction. Here we climbed on a path to the left from the track towards the Col d'Anterne at 2257m. On the way down from the col a golden eagle glided past close above our heads. We passed on the east side of the Lac d'Anterne and then climbed a little before beginning the long zigzaging descent on shaley ground to the Refuge d'Anterne Alfred Wills. This refuge www.refuge-wills.com is named after a Birmingham-born high court judge who had a passion for walking in these hills in the nineteenth century. He was also third president of the Alpine Club. The dortoir has cramped multi-birth bunks in the eves with little headroom. Washing is at a cold tap. The food was good but the poor quality wines available were seriously over-priced. Half board at €47/person in 2009 was expensive for what this refuge offers compared with the many other excellent refuges we have visited. Nevertheless, for this walk it is conveniently sited.

Day 27: Ref. d'Antern Alfred Wills to Ref. de la Golèse (1671m)
23.9km, ascent 1355m, descent 1515m, 7h45
High point the Refuge d'Anterne Alfred Wills 1810m

The view on the way west from the hut is dominated by the massive 4km long limestone cliff of the Rochers de Fiz (above). This towered above us glowing in the direct light of the morning sun. We walked westwards to the Collet d'Anterne, where the snows of Mont Blanc came once more into view across the Col d'Antern (above). The path now enters sparse woodland and turns under the Point de Sales, descending to the much-waterfalled Torrent de Sales (below). We turned north-east at the first falls and descended on a path to the east of the ensuing torrent. This path later meets a lane which it crosses several times before briefly joining it to cross the Pont de Sales. GR5 then leaves the lane and follows the northeast river bank to the Pont des Nants. On the far side of this bridge the GR climbs steeply to the dry rocky Gorges des Tines, which are negotiated easily with the aid of fixed ladders. After descending again to the river at les Faix we crossed the bridge and followed the northeast bank for 2.5 km to a confluence with a tributary – le Glevieux. We walked up this side-stream's east bank and crossed a bridge to make a short detour into the bustling central square of Samoëns.

After a pleasant lunch *al fresco* we returned to the east bank of the Glevieux and GR5. With the exception of one or two short-cuts the onward route followed a quiet mountain lane that heads up through the forest in a generally northern direction. At the 1373m the road becomes a track, emerges from the forest and heads north-east across open alp towards the Col de la Golèse. On this track we were joined by an attractive and friendly Border Collie who remained with us overnight and for part of the following day, before heading for home. The refuge de la Golèse lies a short distance before the col de la Golèse some 100m to the right of the main track www.refuge-golese.com. Shortly after arriving at the refuge we met up with my friend Michael Reth, who had walked over from Champéry to join us on the last 3 stages of the walk to St Gingolph. This excellent refuge provides good food and hot showers. At €36/person half board it was great value.

Day 28: Refuge de la Golèse to Les Brochaux (1576m)
17.2km, ascent 968m, descent 1064m, 6h00
High point les Portes de Hiver 2096m

This walk crosses the border into Switzerland and in this way avoids the high-rise concrete ski resort of Avoriaz. We followed the track over the Col de la Golèse and continued northeast to the International border at the Col de Coux. From there GR5 traverses, still to the northeast, through the cow pastures that fall from the frontier ridge. We stopped for a leisurely lunch at the Lapista mountain restaurant and enjoyed the fine views across the valley to les Dents du Midi (below).

The track taken after lunch passes beneath the Chavanette ski wall and then continues into the next valley. Just after Chaux Palin we took a path that climbs northwards to the Portes de l'Hiver (2096m). On reaching this col there was a clap of thunder and it started to rain. Fortunately after hurriedly skirting to the south of the Lac Vert we were able to shelter at a Refuge until the shower had passed.

It stopped raining after half an hour and we set off westwards crossing back into France at the Col de Chésery. A left fork from GR5 descends steeply to the south to a ski track, which we followed to the right to les Brochaux. There we stayed at the Refuge Abricotine www.refuge-abricotine.com/uk/. This is a pleasant mountain restaurant that has a good bunkroom with hot showers.

Day 29: Les Brochaux to La Chapelle d'Abondance (1230m)
18.7km, ascent 1082m, descent 1638m, 6h30
High point les Mattes 1930m

On this penultimate day of our walk to Lake Geneva we climbed up the broad track that leads to the Col de Bassechaux, rejoining GR5 at the last hairpin bend before the col. After crossing the col we left the road on a path that descends northwards through flower-filled meadows (above) to a col at 1664m. Soon after the path becomes a track it crosses another track and then heads nor-nor-east, climbing gently on the tranquil western side of the Abondance Valley. The views across the valley to the east were of the border ridge and the Ports de Soleil ski area. At 1733m the track winds round the ridge of the Crête de Coincon. Half the group followed a path up this ridge to the summit of Mont de Grange (2432m). From there they took a steep path that leads down to the Chapelle d'Abondance. Michael and I continued along the track on GR5. After rounding the ridge we descended in zigzags before traversing below Mont de Grange. Shortly after the buildings at l'Etrye GR5 leaves the track and zigzags up steep alpine meadows to cowsheds at le Mattes. The sheds are set in a broad almost level meadow, where we rested watching our energetic friends walking up the skyline on the Crête de Coincon. On the far side of the meadow from the cowsheds we headed east-nor-east down a small valley, turning at 1529m to the northeast and continuing our descent through woods on the south side of the Abondance Valley. The path turns right before a stream with a waterfall and then heads for a road that crosses the Abondance river. The waymarks on the far bank show that GR5 has been moved from the route along the road shown on the IGN map to a riverside grassy track on the north bank of the river. This more pleasant option eventually reaches a track that heads up to the valley road a little before la Chapelle d'Abondance. We walked into the village in time for a leisurely lunch.

Just before the centre of the Village we turned north onto the Route de Chevennes. Le Vieux Moulin, the hotel where we were to stay, is a short way up the road on the right. This chalet-style building has balconies on each floor that were decorated with an abundance of red and pink geraniums. The others arrived a little later and were unlucky to catch an isolated shower as they walked through the village. Le Vieux Moulin www.hotel-vieuxmoulin.com/ has comfortable rooms and a good restaurant. It also has an excellent cellar with moderately-priced wines.

Day 30: la Chapelle d'Abondance to St Gingolph (385m)
18.9km, ascent 1843m, descent 2725m, 8h00
High point les Cornettes de Bise 2482m, or
16.3km, ascent1407m, descent 2436m, 6h45
High point the Col de Bise 1915m

The last day in the French Alps continues on GR5 through fine and unspoilt countryside to the shores of lake Geneva. For a final flourish an alternative was taken by the Johns and Andrew over the delicate circuit that traverses the rocky summit of les Cornettes de Bise. This wedge of limestone towers to the east above the GR5. The standard route on the GR goes up the road from the Hotel and then heads into the woods on the left side of the road. At a car park the path goes nor-nor-west climbing through steep alpine meadows to the Pas de la

Bosse. The path to this col is shown below with the Cornettes de Bise in the background.

The route via les Cornets de Bise heads nor-nor-east on a path from the car park and after one zigzag reaches the frontier ridge. There it turns north and zigzags up the ridge through 2000m. The path then traverses north-west under les Roches de Chaudin before regaining the ridge just east of the summit. After passing below and to the south of the summit the path descends steeply to the GR5 at the Pas de la Bosse. The tricky nature of the path on the descent is indicated with red dots on the map.

The rest of the route follows GR5 descending to the Refuge de Bise before climbing to the Col de Bise. From there we looked down 1300m to Lake Geneva. It is worth walking from Briançon to get this view (opposite). The long scenic descent at first winds through beautifully flowered alp and then enters broken forest before reaching the hamlet of la Planche. From there the route turns east-nor-east to the village of Novel where we stopped for a coffee before starting the last section of the walk to St Gingolph. This is on a track that follows the French side of the Morge torrent, as it flows along the border through a wooded gorge to the lake. St Gingolph (pronounced Jango, with a hard o as in go) is no more than a large village that is split by the international frontier and the Morge torrent.

We reached the main road that runs parallel to the lake and turned right crossing the border into Switzerland, before turning down towards the lake and the Hôtel-Restaurant Le Rivage www.rivage.ch. On reaching the lake Michael immediately plunged into the waters, while I sat on the hotel's terrace and applied liquid internally.

This was a wonderful place to end the walk from the Mediterranean to Lake Geneva. It was a warm evening and we found a table on the restaurant's terrace by the lake. We feasted on delicious lake perch and sipped cool rosé wine. There was plenty to talk about at the end of the 30-day journey from the Mediterranean and it was late when we finally made our way to bed.

Breaking the walk at St Gingolph

It is possible to leave St Gingolph by train or boat. The boats go to Vevey or Lausanne. From the Vevey dock it is a 9 minute walk to the railway station and from docks at Ochey there is a local urban railway that links to Lausanne railway station. Trains run frequently from these mainline railway stations to Geneva and Zurich Airports. The branch line from St Gingolph goes to Aigle where it meets the main line going through the Valais.

We chose to take the boat to Vevey and from there got the train to Geneva's Cointrin airport. The boat trip across the lake was a memorable way to finish the walk from the Mediterranean to Lake Geneva. Michael posed us in the stern of the vessel as we were going across the lake and took the happy picture of the long-distance walkers shown below.

JS, Andrew, Ian, JM and JD crossing Lake Geneva from St Gingolph after completing the walk from Menton on the Mediterranean

3 CHAPTER
DAYS 31-42 ST GINGOLPH TO MEIRINGEN
A walk though the Alps of Western Switzerland

This stage of the walk climbs to the east of les Cornettes de Bisse before descending to the Rhône and then walking successively through the Diablerets, Wildhorn, Wildstrubel and Blüemlisalp ranges. The final section covered by this chapter describes a walk past the north faces of 4000m peaks of the Bernese Oberland.

JM, JD and Andrew at the Sefinefurgge on day 40

We had reached St Gingolph in early July 2009 and it was not until September the following year that we returned to continue our walk. This was mainly because I had been hit by a car in a supposedly pedestrian area and landed heavily on my left hip. This joint had failed in the months after the accident and in January 2010 I had the hip relined. It was too early postoperatively to risk a walk in the Swiss Alps in June, with the added concern that we might encounter tricky sections with snow. By the beginning of September there was still 2 weeks before the mountain huts closed for the season and I was ready to take on the first half of our walk across Switzerland.

The selected route across Switzerland is unconventional, for where possible we avoided the popular national cross-Switzerland long distance paths. The exception was near the end of the 2010 walk and start of that in 2011, when for parts of some days we followed significant sections of the Via Alpina. The walk from St Gingolph to Meiringen arguably crosses some of the most varied terrain and scenery of our Alps Traverse. It also includes technically challenging stages matched only by some sections in the Eastern Dolomites. We have no regrets about the route chosen and unreservedly recommend it to others.

The return to St Gingolph (385m)

A Swiss flight took us from Birmingham to Zurich, from where we caught a train to Lausanne. As we approached Bern the white trio of the Eiger, Mönch and Jungfrau stood proudly to the south. The last three days of our planned walk were to be dominated by these high hills. The train climbed through the green meadows that produce Gruyere cheese and then started the steep descent past vineyards to Lake Geneva and Lausanne. During the following days we were to enjoy familiarizing ourselves with the products of such Swiss vineyards.

It was a bright afternoon as we stepped off the train and walked the kilometre or so downhill to the lake and the wharves at Ochey. There was time for an ice cream before catching the 5 pm ferry across the lake to St Gingolph. The ferry-man shouted "San Jango" as we boarded the boat. This time as we moved across the lake towards the steep northern escarpment of the Chablais hills there was nothing moody about the weather and the hills were set against a clear blue sky. A palpable and growing nostalgia was induced by the crossing and the return to St Gingolph and the Rivage hotel with its lakeside restaurant.

Days 31 to 43 from St Gingolph to Meiringen

Day 31: St Gingolph to Taney (1415m)
12.9km, ascent 1571m, descent 584m, 5h30
high point the Pas de Lovenex 1855m

The walk from the St Gingolph to Taney is relatively short, but it makes a delightful day. The steep climb into the limestone hills to the south in good weather has the spectacular backdrop of the azure lake. As the sun rose above the hills behind Montreux there was an amazing clustering of cormorants on the water. These presumably live on fish in the lake and in such numbers must play havoc with the local fishery.

After waiting for a train to pass we crossed the railway and made our way to the southern edge of the village. A signpost there indicates the route to Taney on a path that climbs steeply through woods to la Croix des Dammes. From there a lane leads gently upwards to the south through forest on the east side of the steep valley of the river Morge. After passing through the hamlet of Le Freney we reached a cluster of buildings at Clarive where a jovial man was building a stone wall in front of his chalet. On the far side of the valley we could see the French hill village of Novel. While the previous year Novel appeared somewhat dead, probably because it is mainly used for holidays and weekends this hamlet on the Swiss side is occupied by a lively small community.

After Clarive the lane sweeps round to the left and we followed a new white-red and white waymarked path to the right that is not yet shown on the Swiss 1.25k map. The path heads uphill through the forest and after some time rejoins the road. On coming out of the woods we passed some farm buildings where cheese is sold. From there a stony track makes wide sweeping zigzags up and across a broad meadow. On the third sweep a signpost indicates an indistinct path that heads straight up the grassy hillside to the south. As the meadow steepens, the path winds round to the east and becomes stony. It is a tough, but satisfying climb to the Col de la Croix at 1757m. We rested in clear sunshine at the col, enjoying the view. Across the valley to the west we could see the way we had come down from the Col de Bise to Novel the previous year.

Eventually we set off on a traverse to the south under the rock aiguilles, les Miettes. To the left there is an exquisite view where the hillside falls away steeply from the path to a grass-floored hanging valley with the shallow Lac de Lovenex (opposite). Two limestone outcrops frame the grassy lip of the valley, forming a window through which the blue waters of Lake Geneva can be seen some 1400m below.

Our traverse continued to the Pas de Lovenex at 1850m, where white limestone cliffs rise on each side of the pass, but the way onward was across green closely-grazed meadow grass. To the south les Cornettes de Bise rise another 600m from the far side of the alp. Our path veered east past three small tarns to a well-built stone cattle barn. From there we could see east past les Diablerets to the snowy 4000m peaks of the Bernese Alps 100 km away. A track then led us past a farm, where pigs were wallowing in mud, it then wound down to a point where we could see the beautiful Lac de Taney and its surrounding pointed limestone peaks.

A grassy path now veers right from the track and heads down under a cliff wall to the hamlet of Taney. We feasted on succulent wild raspberries and admired banks of beautiful, but deadly blue monk's hood at the side of this path. Lower down in the meadows above Taney there was a large herd of Simmental cows with bells clanging.

We passed between the fine old wooden chalets of the village and reached the Auberge-Refuge La Vouivre, which overlooks the west end of the lake. At a table on the terrace we soon acquired food and drink and slowly consumed a late lunch in the warm afternoon sunshine. It had been a great start to our walk along the length of Switzerland.

Our room had two double-tiered bunk beds and this was next to a room with hot showers and modern toilets. The shower room separated us from a large dortoir occupied by a party of children. They were a cheerful, but well behaved bunch and were obviously enjoying their trip to the hills. Nevertheless, we were grateful to have our own room. In the evening we ate well and had some excellent local wine. This refuge www.lactaney.com/ is well worth a visit.

Day 32: Taney to Yvorne (445m)
19.1km, ascent 286m, descent 1256m, 5h00
High point le Col des Miots 1496m

The route selected to cross the Rhône starts with a spectacular walk to the village of Mieux and then continues down through fields and woods to Vouvry. This small town is squeezed between the base of steep mountains and the river. From Vouvry it is a relaxing and largely-shaded walk to Yvorne along first the Rhône and then the north bank of the Grand Eau. This ancient village lies in a sea of vineyards on the gentle eastern slopes of the Rhône valley.

The path along the north shore of the Lac de Taney climbs above a cliff before descending to the east end of the lake. There we had a wonderful view back to Taney (above) with reflections of the hills in the still waters of the lake. A track then climbs gently east-nor-east through forest with grassy clearings. Heavy dew on the grass and seed fluff of bronzing rosebay willow-herb glistened in the low morning sunshine. After going through some loops the track reaches a ledge on a rockface, where there is a bench. Below the ledge the rock falls precipitously to the valley floor and beyond is Lake Geneva (opposite).

The track climbs from the rock to a col at 1498m before heading down to the south west, leaving the forest and crossing a grassy alp. On the far side of this meadow the track turns left and enters beech woods before continuing steeply down to the village of Mieux, some 450m below the col. We followed the road to the left through the village and shortly after a hairpin bend turned onto a stony track to the left signed as a footpath to Vouvrey. This leads down through woods crossing the road three times before reaching a bridge across the Fossan torrent. On the far side we followed the south bank of the torrent into the outskirts of Vouvrey, from where we made our way down to the main road that runs parallel to the west bank of the Rhône.

We had a good lunch at an inn on the main road and after this welcome break walked some 0.8km to the north to a metal bridge over the Rhône. On the far bank the route follows a cycle track southwards on a dyke for some 5 km. This was partially shaded and there was a cooling breeze. Ahead were fine views across the river to les Dents du Midi. We turned off the track where the Grand Eau, the river that flows from les Diablerets, meets the Rhône.

As we wandered along the track we could see Yvorne, but the day was hot and we decided to rest on the grass of the dyke that protects the surrounding fields from the Grand Eau in spate. It was a beautiful day and we passed a pleasant half hour reclining in the shade of black poplars. Eventually we got to our feet and wandered along the top of the dyke until we reached the main railway line that passes through the Rhône valley. A track downwards to the left goes to a tunnel under the railway. From there we made our way on a lane and then along the edge of a vineyard to a narrow walled road that leads to the north end of the main street in Yvorne. We passed a series of *caves* belonging to the local vineyards as we made our way southwards towards a small square on the left near the end of the main street. There we came to our lodgings, the Auberge de la Couranne. There was plenty of time to shower and rest before dinner and admire the view back across the valley towards Tany. The Auberge www.aubergedelacouronne.ch has an excellent restaurant with a fine selection of local wines. With the advice of the waitress we were introduced to three of these during our delightful meal on the terrace. There is no doubt that this was one of the more popular stopovers on our walk to Meiringen.

Day 33: Yvorne to les Diablerets (1188m)
18.6km, 1330m ascent, 596m descent, 6h15
High point la Forclaz 1285m

From the hotel we headed down the road towards Aigle, but just outside Yvorne turned left onto a lane that passes through vineyards and rejoins the main road by a bridge across the Grand Eau. After crossing this bridge we made our way round the south-eastern flank of the town before turning towards the fine chateau (above). This is delightfully set in vineyards and was brilliantly lit by the bright morning sunshine. After crossing more vineyards we followed a lane that winds up the southern wooded flank of the valley of the Grand Eau. The well-signposted route climbs gradually to a high point at the pretty village of la Forclaz and then descends on a lane through fields to Vers l'Eglise. We stopped in this village with elegant stone houses and a cobbled main street for a pleasant lunch at the Auberge de l'Ours. It is only a couple of km from Vers l'Eglise to les Diablerets on a lane that runs along the south bank of the Grand Eau. A bridge crosses into the Rue de la Gare in Diablerets and our lodging, the excellent Auberge de la Poste www.aubergedelaposte.ch/, is at the far end of this road.

The town has the feel of a large village, but it is a bustling place. To the south the view is dominated by the mountain also named les Diablerets (below). It is an impressive east to west flake of rock. Apparently winter skiing here is adventurous but not particularly convenient for it involves a trip by bus to the Col du Pillon east of the town to access the cable cars that go up the main mountain. The alternative is to head west to the ski resort at Villars. Andrew arrived at le Diablerets on the train to join us for the next week's walking.

Day 34: les Diablerets to l'Auberge du Sanetsch (2068m)
20.1km, ascent 1272m, descent 557m, 6h30
High point the Auberge du Sanetsch 2053m

Our first task was to climb some 350m eastwards to the Col du Pillon at the head of the valley, before making a descent to the village of Gsteig. The day then ends with a sharp climb of 900m to the Lac de Senin (Sanetsch) where we spent the night.

A left turn from the auberge into the Chemin de la Corbaz led to a track that crosses the Dar, a tributary of the Grande Eau. Here we turned left from the track onto a path, which after a while re-crosses the stream on a rickety suspension bridge before following an up and down course through the woods on the north bank of the stream. Eventually the path comes to an open meadow. On the right is a massive rock face, while our path swings to the north round the edge of a meadow and climbs to the road just before the Col du Pillon.

From the col our route followed the road for about a km and then took a track to the right that passes a dairy – the Fond des Joux, where cheese is sold at the door. The track climbs across a meadow for about 0.6km, where a signpost indicates our path leading down through cow pasture to the east-nor-east. The path becomes more distinct as it enters woods and continues downwards for 1.3km where it joins a stony track. We turned left onto this towards a cable car station. In the car park below the station there is a right turn through a gate to a path that crosses a meadow and descends to a bridge. Once across the bridge the path heads towards some agricultural buildings. The route then turns left down a track and waymarks led us down to and then along the bank of the Rüschbach. As the name of this stream indicates we had now entered German-speaking Switzerland. After a while the route crosses the stream and reaches a road and a recently-built huge wooden chalet restaurant at Heiti, where we had a leisurely lunch.

In the afternoon we walked down the road to the small village of Gsteig and at the junction of 4 roads turned onto a minor road that heads south-east across flat meadows to a cable car station. This cable car provides a fast way up to the Lac de Sanetsch (above), but this was not for us. It was a long, hot, but enjoyable climb in the afternoon sun up the large, green and pleasant cirque to the Auberge/Restaurant du Barrage du Sanetsch www.sanetsch.ch. This is sited at the north end of the lake above the barrage and is once again in French-speaking territory. The large terrace was crowded with people, who were finishing their Sunday lunch before leaving via the cable car, or driving along the narrow road that heads south to Sion. Waitresses in short alpine-style checked cotton frocks were clearing up, but found time to bring us desperately-needed beers. Within an hour the crowds departed and we had the place to ourselves. In the dortoir the mattresses were placed on annoyingly squeaky chipboard. Despite the noise from this base, after an excellent meal with plenty of Vaudois pinot noir wine, we had no difficulty falling asleep.

Day 35: Lac de Senin to Cabane des Audannes (2508m)
13.2km, ascent 1197m, descent 742m, 6h00
High point the Col des Audannes 2890m

This was the day we entered the high hills and the walking on our way to the Cabane des Audannes became considerably more challenging. From the auberge the path leads south along the eastern shore of the lake. It was windless and there were fine reflections of the Sanetschhorn in the morning light (opposite). At the far end of the lake we headed across the meadows that lead up to the Col de Sanetsch shortcutting the loops of the narrow road to Sion in the Rhône Valley. From the col the walk became harder with a steep and delicate climb eastwards up the crest of the Arête de l'Arpille (above). This sharp ridge is composed of compacted grit and feels quite exposed in places. Eventually the gradient lessens and ridge broadens. From here there should be magnificent views of the Alps to the south from Mont Blanc to Monte Rosa. Unfortunately clouds were covering the tops of highest of the peaks, but the prospect was still impressive and most of the 4000m mountains could be identified. The path then traverses the hillside to the right, providing an easy and fast walk to a barren stony valley the Grande Gouilles. The Wildhorn dominates the view ahead while to the right steep scree leads up to the Col des Audannes. After passing to the right of a lake we crossed a stream and started zigzagging up the scree towards this col. Eventually the "path" comes to a couloir where a fixed, or rather semi-fixed, rope led the way up loose rock to a shallow scree platform. On reaching the top of the rope it was clear that the steel rod to which this was tied could easily be removed by

gently lifting it upwards. This was a clear warning to be wary when using "fixed" ropes.

We crossed the scree platform from the top of the first rope to the foot of the final climb to the Col des Audannes (opposite). This climb is on unstable rock and is protected by fixed rope, chains and ladders. All these aids appeared to be securely fixed, unlike the rope in the previous couloir. The top of the col at 2890m is the highest point we had yet crossed on our route from Menton.

The way on from the col descends east-south-east along a ridge to the Col la Selle at 2705m. From there the descent continues east on delightfully grippy rock pavement with clear waymarking to the Cabane des Audannes www.audannes.ch. This is a modern hut with a warm day-room on the first floor and a large, well-lit dormitory above. The mattresses in the multi-birth bunks were well-spaced. Washing facilities on the ground floor are clean, but offer no more than cold taps above stainless steel sinks. The long-drop toilets are outside.

Day 36: Cabane des Audannes to Iffigenalp (1584m)
11.7km, ascent 636m, descent 1544m, 5h00
High point the Col des Eaux Froides 2648m

This high level walk passes back into German-speaking Switzerland. It was one of the few days on our Alps traverse where it rained from start to finish of the walk. It would be good to repeat this interesting day in fine weather.

From the cabane the route climbs north-east to the Col des Eaux Froides (above). Foreshortening makes this look frighteningly steep from the hut, but it proved straightforward, even in the rain. On the other side of the col the descent is relatively gentle before the route heads up rocks to the left. Some scrambling follows on rough limestone that provides good grip even in the wet and the well-waymarked route is entertaining rather than difficult.

After a while the route joins a path coming up from the Lac de Tenechet and follows this to the northwest before going right onto a path that climbs to a col. There is then another easy scramble down rocks to a grassy alp. On the far side of this meadow the path climbs to a small lake at the Plan des Roses (2386m), from where there is a long gentle walk on a broad path up to the Col du Rawil.

The descent from this col is northwards down a large grassy cwm, but the path becomes more exciting after passing a cowshed, marked on the map as the Blatthütte. This spectacularly and miraculously winds its way down the massive cliffs to the south of Iffigenalp. The path is well made, but sufferers from vertigo should avoid this route. After the long and unrelenting descent the path reaches level ground at Iffigenalp. The Berghaus Iffigenalp www.iffigenalp.ch/ lies on this pleasant pasture and is an excellent place to stay. The restaurant serves good food and their welcome, on our arrival after this damp day's outing cheered us considerably. Comfortable bedrooms are located in a separate wooden chalet with beds as opposed to bunks. There is also a welcome hot shower.

Day 37: Iffigenalp to Engstligenalp (1937m)
14.5km, ascent 1478m, descent 1111m, 6h50
High point the Ammertepass 2443m

It was overcast but not raining as we started the walk heading northeast down the lane that serves Iffigenalp. This narrow single track road is regulated by a novel traffic light system that allows ascent to start for 20 minutes an hour and descent for a similar time with 10 minutes to complete the passage each way.

Some 0.5km from the Berghaus we took a path to the right that crosses a stream and heads nor-nor-east in zigzags up a steep pasture to a cowshed. Then our route veered to the right uphill on a track that gradually wound round to the east before crossing a broad col. The descent into the Rezliberg valley is on a path that is steep in places. Eventually this levels out and joins a track that follows the north bank of the river Simme. Large waterfalls (opposite) swollen by the previous day's rain were feeding this boiling river.

After passing some chalets on the left we crossed the Simme by a footbridge and the path on the far side led to two more chalets, one of which is a restaurant, although it was not open. From there we followed a track that crosses the Ammertebach just before its confluence with the Simme.

At this point a track leading to the right took us into the Ammertetäli valley. The path up to the Ammertepass is well marked. At first it crosses and recrosses the Ammertebach. It then climbs steeply up a headwall to the left of the stream that tumbles out of a hanging valley. After passing a precariously located shack the path enters the grass-floored Ammerte Shafberg where sheep were grazing. It is easy walking up the base of this hanging valley but then the path starts to climb steeply in zigzags up a grassy buttress, which is exposed in places. This leads to a scree-filled cirque, where there is a brief respite as the path zigzags safely up the scree to the left. Finally there is an exposed and uncomfortable traverse on an unstable, narrow and angled path (next page). We were relieved to reach the Ammertegrat and rested there for a while before following this ridge north-westwards to the

Amertepass. A notice at the pass warns of the dangers of the path we had just come up.

From the col the path descends without difficulty to the grassy Engstligenalp. After the ground has flattened off the path crosses a river and heads north east. It was misty here and we were glad when the Berghaus Bärtschi www.engstligenalp.ch/12.0.html, which is on the left of the path, emerged from the gloom. This comfortable Berghaus provided us with simple bedrooms, plenty of hot water, drying facilities and excellent food.

Day 38: Engstligenalp to Oeschinensee (1593m)
16.7km, ascent 1025m, descent 1394m, 6h18
High point the Schedlsgrätli 2512m

After the mist of the previous evening it was a magical clear crisp morning and the hills surrounding the Engstligenalp were dusted with fresh snow (below). We set off for the base of the Artelgrat, which forms the east ridge of the pyramidal Tschingellochtighore. A good path zigzags up to this ridge and on reaching its grassy crest we emerged from the shade and climbed the ever steepening path up the pyramid. The north-west flank of this hill, which we were planning to traverse, looked frighteningly steep. In the event this appearance was due to foreshortening and the narrow path that leads across this face presented no serious difficulties despite a light covering of snow. As we emerged from the shade of the pyramid into the warm sunshine of the north ridge the view was formidable and we spent several minutes enjoying this lofty perch. There was a steep descent of some 600m to the floor of the green Inner Üschene hanging valley. We followed the narrow road here past a number of farms, before descending on a path beside the waterfalled Alpbach to the lower valley and the Kander River.

At Eggeschwand we had a sandwich on the lawn in front of an inn. After lunch our route crossed to the west bank of the Kander river and followed this to Kandersteg. There we recrossed the river and passed under the railway. On the far side of the main road a track climbs east through woods to join the road to the Oeschinensee, which is closed to non-resident traffic. This road climbs steeply to the hotel by the lake, some 400m above Kandersteg. On arriving there we refreshed ourselves on the terrace, admiring the massive cliffs on the far side of the Oeschinensee that rise to the snow-capped peaks of the Blüemlisalp (below). The Hotel Oeschinensee www.oeschinensee.ch has a bunk room and hot showers. After a meal in the restaurant we spent a pleasant evening in the comfortable sitting room in front of the blazing wood-burning stove.

Day 39: Oeschinensee to Gspaltenhornhütte (2455m)
11.5km, ascent 1931m, descent 1069m, 7h22
High point the Hotürli pass 2778m

It had been raining most of the night, but while we ate our breakfast some blue sky appeared, the precipitation ceased and the weather continued to improve throughout the day. We set out along the north shore of the lake and soon were climbing over a cliff that rises from the lake. From the top of this rock the path starts to wind away from the lake up steep pasture, passing the three chalets at Underbärgli. There was then a scramble through some rocks to reach a hanging valley, where the path climbs up its north side. Occasionally, when gaps appeared in the mist, we had glimpses of the Blüemlisalp glaciers. Around 2400m the path reaches a long rocky ledge on the top of a cliff that drops to the valley floor. At the end of this ledge the path starts to climb round the head of the valley on steep fine black fractured shale. In places wooden steps have been placed to provide security, but this is no place for the vertiginous. We were in mist when we reached the safety of the rocky platform at the Hohtürli pass, a gap in the ridge just below the Blüemlisalphütte.

The way down from this pass is also vertiginous. The path again is scraped out of unreassuring fine black shale. There were some dubious frayed fixed ropes, which we avoided and some well made wooden steps that did provide assistance. The route here is on the Via Alpina and we met a couple of parties ascending as we picked our way down the hillside. Fortunately these encounters were not at delicate sections of the descent. Some 720m below the col we came to a signpost. The Via Alpina continues downwards. We turned right on a path that traverses towards the glacier below the Gespaltenhornhütte. This traverse crosses a large grassy cirque before descending through boulders to the massive stone-covered Gamchigletscher. There are impressive ice caves in this glacier and at one point we crossed a steel bridge over a chasm in the ice with a torrent far below in its base. Fortunately the route across this glacier is well marked and straightforward. On the far side there is a long climb up to the Gespaltenhornhütte www.gspaltenhornhuette.ch. This is hidden until the last moment, when suddenly the hut comes into view. It is delightfully perched on a rock ledge high above the head of the Gamchigletscher (below). Beyond lies of the eastern end of the

Blüemlisalp range. This spectacular range is seen in full sunlight in the photo (opposite) taken the following day from the Sefinefurgge. As one would expect the facilities in the Gespaltenhornhütte are basic, but we enjoyed our stay, for the hospitality is excellent.

Day 40: Gspaltenhornhutte to Lauterbrunnen (805m)
16.8km, ascent 764m, descent 2354m, 7h00
High point the Sefinefurgge 2612m

It was a beautifully clear still morning as we set off for the Sefinefurgge pass on an airy path that traverses high above the Gamchigletscher. After rounding the east ridge of the Bütlasse the path moves onto less steep ground climbing gradually to a ridge. Then we circled round the head of a steep cirque to a rocky outcrop above the Sefinefurgge (page 65). From here the northern high peaks of the Bernese Oberland came into view, their snow-capped summits silhouetted in the clear morning sunshine (above, the peaks left to right are the Wetterhorn, Eiger Mönch and Jungfrau).

Behind us the Blüemlisalp peaks, which had been shy in the mist on the previous day, gleamed against the clear blue sky (opposite). We were alone on this outcrop and took our time immersing ourselves in the alpine splendour. Eventually we pressed on and had to negotiate a short, but tricky descent to the col, where we rejoined the Via Alpina. From there it is a long walk, traversing on the steep south and west flanks of the Shilthorn on the way to Mürren. With every bend in the path a new more spectacular view of the giants of the Oberland presented. After we had passed the Rotstokhütte the green flowered hillside fell away to our right at an ever increasing angle, emphasizing the massive snowy cliffs on the other side of the valley. On reaching the Wasenegg ridge, which comes down from the Shilthorn, there is a steep, but safe descent in tight zigzags to the mountain restaurant at Spilboden, where we had lunch. We then headed north-west through Mürren and followed the mountain railway out of this large but pretty

car-free village. About 1km west of Mürren we took a path that winds down through the woods to Lauterbrunnen. Just above this town two sets of mountain-bikers charged past us at great speed. It was fortunate that there was space in this section of the path for us to get out of the way, for they were barely in control and did not slow as they went by.
On reaching in the main street of Lauterbrunnen we turned right and soon reached the modern Valley Hostel, where we had booked lodging. This hostel www.valleyhostel.ch is located below the main street on the left. The warden allocated us space in a dormitory with 4 twin bunk beds. We discovered we were to share our dormitory with 4 Japanese ladies. They were in their bunks before we got back after dinner and

were still there when we left the following morning. Whether this was due to modesty or indolence remains unclear. The hostel fee at 28.00 Ch Fr per person/night including tax, bedding and a hot shower has to be extraordinary value for Switzerland.

We went out for dinner at the Oberland Restaurant, where we marked Andrew's last night with us on this walk and the memorable day we had had on the hills. It was a warm evening and we sat on the terrace eating an excellent *beuf bourguignon* with suitable liquid accompaniments.

Day 41: Lauterbrunnen to Grindelwald (1120m)
20km, ascent 1450m, descent 1250m, 7h40
High point the Kleine Scheidegg 2061m

We said goodbye to Andrew at the railway station in Lauterbrunnen and then crossed the river. It was a long strenuous walk from there to the Kleine Scheidegg. Most people visit this col using the mountain railways that run from Lauterbrunnen and Grindelwald. The railway also goes on from the Kleine Scheidegg to the Jungfrau Joch. Happily the trains leave the approaches to the Kleine Scheidegg relatively empty, but the area around the station at the col itself was unpleasantly crowded.

The route to Wengen is through forest on a track climbing at a steady steep angle through regular zigzags. It was still early as we passed through the narrow streets of this large village and few people were around. After Wengen the track heads south climbing across alpine meadows, where skiers abound in the winter and through small woods. The north face of the Eiger was becoming ever more prominent as we climbed higher. It was a shock to arrive at the Kleine Scheidegg, for the crowd transported there by the railway was immense and stifling. We quickly headed away from the station to a restaurant a small distance to the north of the junction. There in relative peace we sat on the terrace and ate lunch out of sight of the station, but with a fine view of the Eiger's North Wall (opposite), which had only a scanty covering of snow.

The postprandial stroll down to Grindelwald started in good weather through the fields beneath the Eiger. At one point we passed a chalet where an outdoor religious service was being held. By the time we approached the river at Grund the afternoon sun had gone and the clouds looked threatening. I was beginning to feel weary and did not relish the prospect of the 200m climb through Grindelwald to our lodging. As we reached the station in the centre of town it started to rain. So the final ascent along steep lanes to the Terassenweg, where our lodging was located was completed at speed.

We arrived at the Naturfreundehaus hot, wet and exhausted http://naturfreundehaeuser.ch/grindelwald. We were each given a tankard of cooling beer before being shown to our twin-bedded rooms. The showers were wonderful and we came down for dinner considerably refreshed. A good meal was served and the selection of wines was excellent. The Naturfreundehaus at Grindelwald is strongly recommended.

Day 42: Grindelwald to Meiringan (600m)
23.0km, ascent 1100m, descent 1550m, 7h20
High point the Grosse-Scheidegg 1962m

The Terrassenweg contours above Grindelwald, giving a good start on the way to the Grosse Scheidegg. It was not raining when we set off, but the clouds were threatening and by the time we joined the road from the Centre of Grindelwald it had started to rain. Despite this it was a pleasant walk up to the Grosse Scheidegg. I got into a good rhythm by humming the theme from the first movement of

Beethoven's Pastoral Symphony. As we approached the pass the rain turned to snow and it was still snowing when we reached the berghaus, where we stopped to have a cup of coffee.

When we emerged after our drink, as in the symphony, the sky miraculously cleared and the sun came out. The view back to the west was unbelievably fine. The massive rock flake of the Eiger was powdered with fresh snow and a plume of cloud dazzlingly lit by the bright sunlight streamed from its sharp Mitellegi ridge (above).

Invigorated by this view and the coffee stop we headed down the Reichenbachtal. Just then a powder avalanche of newly-fallen snow hurtled down the north face of the Wetterhorn. The precipitation held off while we walked down the wet path towards the Rosenlaui hotel. This is at the top of the section of the road from Meiringen that is open to vehicles of the public. Only post-busses are allowed to continue to the Grosse Scheidegg. J D and I had a very good cold lunch in the elegant dining room of this period hotel. It probably dates from the second half of the 19th century. We waited for the other two Johns, who were some way behind us, but they did not stop.

After lunch we continued to the head of the Reichenbach falls where Sherlock Holmes and Moriarty are fabled to have fought with a fatal outcome for Holmes. We admired the falls, before returning to their head and continuing from there down the Via Alpina to Meiringen. There we joined the other Johns, who were drinking beers in sunshine in front of our hotel. Their early arrival was not simply due to missing lunch. They had also taken the cable railway from the bottom of the falls to the valley. I am pleased to report that they remedied this loss of continuity in the Grand Traverse of the Alps before walking on from Meiringen the following year.

The Hotel Victoria www.victoria-meiringen.ch is a comfortable three star establishment with a gastronomic restaurant where we enjoyed their extensive and excellent taster menu celebrating our completion of the third stage of our alpine traverse. It was a great place to finish the walk and we had no hesitation in booking there for our return visit to Meiringen when we were to continue our walk the following year.

Days 43-56 Meiringen to Pontresina

4 CHAPTER
DAYS 43-56 MEIRINGEN TO PONTRESINA
A walk though the Alps of Eastern Switzerland

The Alps of Eastern Switzerland

After the second day walking eastwards from Meiringen the backdrop of peaks over 4000m in the Bernese Oberland gives way to somewhat lower, but still charming hills that are wonderful to walk through. This part of Switzerland tends not to be listed in the brochures of tour companies or macho climbing magazines. So much the better, for here we found solitude in beautiful hills and a warm welcome from hostelries and huts that expected local rather than international customers. Here we heard Rumantsch, Switzerland's fourth tongue with its five or so dialects and confusing variability of signposts. The flowers in the alpine meadows, as always in late June and early July were magnificent. All this changed on the last day, when on topping the Fuorcla Surlej we came face to face with the brilliant snowy peaks of the Bernina Range. Inevitably this view of the most easterly of the 4000m peaks was associated with increased tourist activity as we walked down towards Pontresina. Nevertheless, as tourist towns go Pontresina has considerable style and proved a fine place to finish the fourth stage of our walk across the Alps.

Day 43: Meiringen to Engstlenalp (1834m)
20km, ascent 1854m, descent 621m, 8h30
High point the Balmeregghorn 2255m

The Via Alpina route beyond Meiringen becomes considerably less busy. It makes its way to Engstlenalp via the Planplatten ridge and the Balmeregghorn involving a walk that is comparable in height gain and distance to the long trek from Briançon to Névache on the first day of the second stage of our traverse of the Alps in 2009.

It was overcast when we set out from the hotel and remained so all day, but the cloud level was high and it was dry. The well-signed series of tracks and paths that lead to Planplatten presented no technical difficulties. Twists and zigzags on the way up from time to time gave a view west to the cloud-capped precipitous north wall of the Wetterhorn, which rises from the south side of the Grosse Scheidegg, the last high col on our previous year's walk. From the crest of the ridge at Planplatten we could see the path ahead where it traverses across the steep grassy hillside on the north side of the Gental. On the other side of this deep valley rise the rocky peaks of the Wendenstöcke and Titlis. The restaurant at the top of the Planplatten cable car provides a convenient stop for lunch. From there the path drops to a col and then climbs before traversing across the steep grassy hillside beyond (below). Fortunately the path continues to be broad, for the drops to the right in places are vertiginous. At the end of the traverse the path descends to a shallow hanging valley before starting the stiff climb to the summit of the Balmeregghorn. The top of this hill is rounded and on its north side is the terminal of a ski lift that rises from the shores of the Melchsee. Insensitive development at Frutt on the far side of this lake has damaged the view in that direction. The deep and peaceful Gental to the south and the ridge heading eastwards are far more pleasing.

It is relatively easy going along the ridge after the Balmeregghorn with only an occasional short ascent. Mountain-bikers were out in force on the ridge this Saturday. They were heading westwards and passing them was generally not a problem.

The hotel at Engstlenalp becomes visible when it is still at least an hour's walk away. Soon after the first sighting the ridge broadens and descends to the Tanensee. The buildings and inn at the far end of this lake are rather bleak and we were glad to have decided to continue to the distinctly more beautiful Engstlenalp.

To get there we followed a path that winds round the west end of a rock face and then descends across the base of this cliff using a steep path cut into the rock. A safety cable is fitted here although it was not needed in the good conditions we were enjoying. Below the rocks the fantastic flowers along the path included crimson vetches, St Bernard Lilies and a host of Fragrant Orchids (below).

It had been a long first day and we were glad to reach the hotel, where we had booked into the bunkhouse www.engstlenalp.ch/. This feeling of relief was reinforced when it started to rain hard soon after our arrival.

The hotel is an elegant late 19th century building, while the bunkhouse is a basic old wooden chalet at the back of the hotel. Fortunately we had a small bunk room to ourselves, for the main dormitory was occupied by a group of schoolboys, who indulged in a treble cacophony well into the night. Their minders seemed to be more interested in drinking in the hotel than looking after their charges. The hotel has a good dining room, but their price of six Swiss francs for a litre of filtered local spring water was excessive, although their other charges seemed reasonable.

Day 44: Engstlenalp to Stäffelialp (1393m)
8.5km, ascent 872m, descent 1313m, 6h30
High point the Jochpass 2207m

The rain had gone and it was a warm clear cloudless day. From the front of the hotel we could see the high snow-capped summits of the eastern Bernese Oberland shimmering in the morning sun. The photograph below shows from left to right: the Finsterarhorn, Lauteraarhorn, Schreckhorn, Rosenhorn, Mittlehorn and Wetterhorn).

We set off on the Via Alpina, which at first is a track along the north side of the Engstlensee. The deep blue sky reflected in the lake contrasted both with the snow-tipped rocky peaks behind and the flower-studded green alp. After the lake we continued on a path that climbs eastwards on the north flank of the valley to the Jochpass. This broad col is a junction of several ski lifts in the Titlis system and has a Berghaus. From this busy junction a path descends northwards zigzagging down through flower-rich meadows and then grass-covered cliffs to the Trübesee. We walked eastwards along the shore of the lake to the road below the Trübesee lift station from where a steep zigzagging path spectacularly, but safely, leads down the cliff below the cable car. At the base of the cliff we crossed the Gerschni cow pasture on a low grassy dyke that led to the road at Vorder Stafel. Here the restaurant provides a good stop for lunch.

After a relaxing meal on the sundrenched terrace we continued on the Via Alpina as a track that crosses meadows before descending steeply through woods towards Engleberg. At about 1120m there is a path that short-cuts the Via Alpina by heading eastwards down to the Engleberger river some way upstream of the town. There a well made track follows the river's south bank. After passing to the right of a golf course this winds round to the north and crosses the river to rejoin the Via Alpina. It was a long hot, but worthwhile haul from there up the valley in the afternoon sun to the Staffelialp. This beautiful alp is surrounded by rocky peaks with hanging glaciers (above) and waterfalls. We stayed at the Staffelialp Gîte-Restaurant in their modern and clean bunk house. They still seem to have no website or email in 2014 and we booked by 'phone (+41-(0)41637/4511). Edith and Richard Arnold, who run this delightful Bergrestaurant, speak excellent English. They spent some time chatting with us after a supper that included delicious goat and cow cheese made with milk from their animals that graze on the Staffelialp.

Day 45: Stäfellialp to Erstfeld (472m)
19.3 km, ascent 1077m, descent 1998m, 7h15
High point the Surenenpass 2291m

We climbed up the valley past the Stauber waterfall, where mauve Martagon Lillies were thriving in the spray from the thundering cascade. At the top of the falls a hanging valley with rich grazing and large numbers of cattle stretched to the northeast. Both sides of this upper valley are defended by continuous massive rock faces that are not bridged by walking paths. After a small chapel at Blackenalp the valley turns eastwards and a good path took us past drifts of alpenrose to the headwall below the Surenenpass.

It was a delightful temperature at the col with fantastic views back down to the rockface of Titlis at the end of the valley. The way forward showed an apparently endless series of mountains stretching to the east that we were going to walk through over the next 12 days.

On the far side of the pass we lost about 180 vertical metres before traversing on a good path across a large scree slope to the start of the Grat ridge (opposite looking back to the Surenenpas). Although this ridge has mainly grassy sides, in places these are quite steep but never frighteningly so. The prospects from the ridge on this clear sunny day were magnificent. On both sides of the path alpine flowers were in full bloom, while 1400m below the ridge on the left the blue waters of Vierwald-Stättersee (below) stretched northwards to the other limbs of Lake Lucerne.

The ridge eases at Rütli where we had lunch on the terrace of a peaceful and pleasant hotel/restaurant. We then continued down through magnificent floral meadows, passing the cable car station at Brüsti where we turned right and soon left the Via Alpina for the last time. Our path then headed westwards to a small lake in the floor of the Waldnachter Valley. From this lake we walked back on the other side of the valley to a dramatic and steep 800m descent on an exciting but well made path. This winds down the southern rim of the Blockitobel canyon. The last sections of the path before Erstfeld required careful map reading. On reaching the valley floor there was a short walk along the west bank of the Reusse river to a bridge that leads into the railway town of Erstfeld.

After passing under the railway we turned right. The Frohsinn, where we were to stay, is the second hotel on the left. The temperature outside in the shade was about 30°C so the 22°C in the hotel hall was welcome and further relief came from cold half-litre glasses of beer served before we went upstairs for a much-needed bath. The Frohsinn www.frohsinn-erstfeld.ch/ is a functional hotel that has comfortable rooms and provides filling meals. It is a good stopover both for walkers and the railway enthusiast.

Erstfeld's busy railway is on the way to the St Gothard tunnel. The hotel owner is a railway buff and has pictures and models of trains everywhere as well as the real thing across the road. The tracks at Erstfeld apparently carry more than 200 trains a day. These glide along the lines making remarkably little noise and caused us no disturbance in our rooms at the back of the hotel where we slept well.

Day 46: Erstfeld to Etzlihütte (2052m)
17.5km, ascent 1760m, descent 180m, 7h15
High point the Etzlihütte 2052m

The first part of this walk follows the broad and fast-flowing river Reusse upstream. This is mainly on a cycle track and crosses the river twice. Despite the proximity to the busy motorway as this highway has noise-deflecting walls the sound of the river dominates. Consequently we had a surprisingly pleasant riverside walk.

About half way to Amsteg our route crossed the river by a road bridge and then continued upstream on the far bank past extensive drifts of Evening Primroses. A small suspension bridge took us back over the river into the village of Amsteg, where we turned right past another bridge hoping to find the start of the Jacobsweg Gaubünden, a regional footpath. We missed this, but a little further on a bergweg sign identified an alternative route that leads up the hill at the back of the village. This steep path twisted through pine woods. After a while it became steeper and seemed to be petering out when happily it joined the more-distinct Jacobsweg Gaubünden. This main path continues to climb steeply up the northern lip of the Bristantobel gorge and eventually comes out of the woods onto a sloping alp above the cliff-edge of the gorge. The path crosses this airy meadow before entering the hamlet of Frentschenberg, where we were glad to rest on a shaded low wall after the strenuous climb from Amsteg.

From the village we walked down a track to a lane that leads to the road up the Maderanertal valley. After entering the village of Cholplatz we crossed a road bridge over the boiling Cärlestelenbach and at the top of the road on the far side came to the mouth of the Etzlibach.

Our route from there followed a grassy track on the west bank of this substantial frothing torrent. Soon the track turned away from the river and we took a waymarked path to the left climbing in zigzags up a steep alp for some 15 minutes. After entering coniferous forest the incline eased and then a short descent led to a bridge over the Etzlibach. On the far side of the torrent a gravel road leads up the Etzlital. Gradually this road approaches and then crosses the torrent before winding round to a dairy. We followed a track that leaves this road just after the second bridge over the Etzlibach. This track zigzags up the slope below a hanging valley. The flowers here and the view back down the valley to the Gross Windgällen were special (below).

On reaching the hanging valley the path winds upwards round its western flank. It then zigzags up the headwall past two thundering waterfalls to a second hanging valley where alpenrose were in full bloom. The path winds across the flat base of this valley between the crystal-clear Etzlibach and granite outcrops before reaching the base of a rocky ridge, where the path turns to the right and climbs steeply up this ridge to the beautifully-sited Etzlihütte.

It had been a tough climb to the hut in the hot sunshine and we greedily ate calorie-restoring lunches and drank cool water from the spout that feeds a trough on the hut's terrace. The rest of the afternoon was spent lazing in the sun. This pleasant and welcoming Swiss Alpine Club hut www.etzlihuette.ch is well worth the tough walk to get there. It was a beautiful evening and the rock peeks surrounding the hut were magnificent in the light of the setting sun (below)

Day 47: Etzlihütte to Mutschnengia (1405m)
16km, ascent 841m, descent 1508m, 6h00
High point the Crüzlipass 2347m

The next morning we made our way back down to the Etzlibach and rejoined the Jacobsweg Gaubünden. After crossing the stream by a log bridge the path heads eastwards, climbing to the north flank of the Crüzlital. The previous evening we had eyed the granite boulder field that covers the floor of this high valley with apprehension and had anticipated a boulder-hopping pull to the Crüzlipass. Fortunately, by climbing to the north the path avoids making a way through the granite boulders on the valley floor and the walk to the Crüzlipass in the cool clear morning air was a joy. It is worth lingering at this rocky and remote pass. We had left the popular Swiss Alps and were finding wonderful solitude that had not been a feature of our days on the Via Alpina.

The sharp descent into the Val Strem uses a well-made path and once on the valley floor this path continues on the west bank of the Strem. There is a beautiful series of waterfalls that tumble down smooth rocks into inviting pools. Again the late June flowers were magnificent. At the 1573m point our route crossed the river and followed a grassy track that traverses out of the valley before descending on a ski run to the outskirts of the small town of Sedrun. Here the Jacobsweg turns left, while our route continued southeast through the town.

We stopped to have coffee and cake in a hotel in the main street and after this break followed a road that leads past gravel workings to a bridge that crosses the deep gorge of the Rein Anterior. Over the next nine days we were to cross several of the headwaters of the Rhein (spelt Rein on the 1:25k Swiss Maps of this region).

On the far side of the gorge we turned left on a road that goes down to a bridge over a side stream before climbing through woods to the outskirts of the village of Cavoria. We continued on the road, which narrows and later becomes a track, gradually climbing eastward up the hillside to a col where there is a pond, with a quirky visual sign prohibiting bathing. Clouds had been building as we made our way to the col and now there were rumbles of thunder. We started to walk faster making our way down the steep alpine meadows that lead to the small village of Mutschnengia. The rain only started after we had arrived at the Hotel/Pension Cuntera www.hotel-cuntera.ch and we were in time for a late lunch. Our comfortable rooms were in a newly-refurbished basement extension of this pleasant and peaceful hotel.

Day 48: Mutschnenia to Camona da Medel (2524m)
12.6km, ascent 1766m, descent 630m, 6h30
High point on the afternoon excursion the Piz Caschleglia 2936m

It had been raining most of the night and the clouds were down over the high ridge we had planned to traverse on our way to the Medelser Hütte or Camona da Medel. Consequently we decided to take the more direct route via the Val Plattas to the col that is described by the wardens of the hut as "the nicest fuorcla in the alps". With views from the hut shown on the photo above that was taken after breakfast the following day, it is hard to argue with this claim. This direct route was short enough to leave the possibility of bagging a peak in the afternoon if the weather improved.

We started on the road that zigzags down to the valley floor and then walked up to the large village of Curaglia. This is working agricultural Switzerland with no sign of hotels or tourists, apart from us. The way up to the Val Plattas is well signposted and a footpath shortcuts the zigzags of the lane leading to this valley. The Rein da Medel was on our left as we climbed through pastures to the large flat-bottomed hanging valley – the Crap Alo. At the entrance to the valley we crossed a wooden bridge over the river and soon started to climb the left flank of the valley to the Fuorcla da Lavaz where the Camona da Medel (Medelserhütte) is located www.medelserhuette.ch.

After we had had some lunch the conditions were sufficiently good to justify an attempt at the 2935m Piz Caschenleglia. This rocky outcrop is the high point on the ridge running north from the Fuorcla da Lavaz and is shown opposite in the photograph taken the following day from the Fuorcla Sura da Lavaz. It is the leftmost peak in the background. The route to the top follows the crest of the ever steepening ridge. The pre-summit is reached by a short rock scramble and then from the far side of a small col the summit is reached by another scramble that this time is protected by fixed chains.

Because the Camona da Medel is on the fuorcla there is a problem trapping water and consequently this is a scarce commodity in the hut. We had a good meal and then enjoyed the evening sunshine with ever improving views. A Steinbok miraculously made its way down a seemingly near-vertical cliff on the far side of the fuorcla. The hospitality provided by Barbara Fischer and Michael Ziefle, the wardens of the Camona da Medel, is exceptional and they give excellent advice about the local hills. Both the hut and fuorcla are well worth a visit, not least for the walk on from there.

Day 49: Camona da Medel to Camona da Terri (2170m)
11.9km, ascent 685m, descent 1037m, 5h40
High point the Fuorcla Sura da Lavaz 2703m

Although the distance and height gain of this walk are modest it is a day of continued interest in magnificent isolated mountain scenery. This excellent route via the Fuorcla Sura da Lavaz is marked on the Swiss 1:25k maps by broken dashes, but is not listed as a route or hiking trail.

From the hut there is a steep descent eastwards to boulder fields 340m below the fuorcla. Blue and white waymarks then lead over granite boulders into the high valley that separates the Piz Medel from the Piz Gaglianera. About a third of the way up the valley the hopping from boulder to boulder ends on reaching the Glatscher da Lavaz. We saw no crevasses on this relatively shallow glacier and scalloping of the snow's surface made going safe and relatively easy. Steeper snow above the glacier leads to the pass (previous page). It was not difficult to kick steps here and the run-out in the event of a slip was in no way daunting.

The Fuorcla Sura da Lavaz gives a wonderful sense of the remote high hills and we lingered there for some time in the bright sunshine. Despite the southern aspect, the descent had long patches of snow, which we ran and slithered down, avoiding more hopping between granite boulders. On arriving at a small tarn we picked up the path that leads down to the Greina Pass.

Shortly after this broad pass the path splits and we took the left fork that runs along the north side of the valley. Eventually, after a short scramble, protected by a chain, the path splits once more. Again we took the left fork and headed northwards over a pass. The Camona di Terri (Terrihütte) photographed opposite www.terrihuette.ch/ lies on a grassy bluff about 100m below this pass.

The Terrihütte is large, which is fortunate, for it was almost full on this Friday night in late June. We were looked after well and the 5 of us were lucky enough to be allocated a small seven-birth bunk room to ourselves. Although there was only cold water, unlike the previous night there was plenty of it.

Day 50: Camona da Terri to Vella (1262m)
22.4km, descent 965m, descent 1880m, 7h30
High point the Pass Diesrut 2428m

This is a long day that follows parts of sections 3 and 4 of the Alpine Passes trail. We had walked the 34th and last section of this trail between St Gingolph and Tanney at the start of the previous year's walk. Unlike the Via Alpina we met almost no other walkers on any of these three sections of this trail.

After reaching the bottom of the bluff on which the Terrihütte is perched there was a sharp climb of some 125m over rocks and a section with steep hard-frozen snow. Near the mid-point on this ascent a small tarn gave magnificent reflections of the hills north of the hut (opposite). After the climb there is a steep descent to a narrow bridge without hand-holds (next page) over the river just before it enters the precipitous gorge of the Rein da Sumvitg. On the far side of the river the path climbs a fragmented ridge, before the gradient eases as it winds towards the broad flat Pass Diesrut.

From this high point we walked down through pastures to the village of Vrin almost 1000m below the pass. The route then traverses on the north-western flank of the valley of the river Glogn. Before Vrin there is a section on mountain road where hay making was in full swing on the adjacent steep meadows. Soon after Vrin we veered off to the left on a track through woods that undulates well above the road.

This is a pleasant walk and the intervening meadows between the woodland displayed an amazing variety of flowers. There are three short sections above and to the north of the village of Lumbrein where the route again joins a mountain road. At the third of these encounters the Alpine Passes route goes up the road to the left, while our route followed the road down-hill to the northeast. After about half a km at a hairpin to the right and we followed a path straight ahead through cow pasture. This path rises a little before descending to the village of Vella. It meets a road on the outskirts of Vella that passes a football pitch. From the end of the pitch we could see the Hotel Pellas by a ski lift on the other side of a meadow www.pellas.ch/Home.413.0.html.

It was a relief to sit on the hotel's terrace and drink cool beer at the end of this long warm walk. Our accommodation was in a comfortable spacious bunk room in the basement of the hotel, which we had to ourselves. This dormitory seems to be mainly used in the winter by skiers, for the hotel is at the base of a lift system. There was unlimited hot water and the drying facilities were excellent, so we caught up with our laundry. The restaurant of this comfortable and modestly-priced stopover was also good.

Day 51: Vella to Glaspass (1846m)
27.4km, ascent 2347m, descent 1741m, 10h45
High point the Güner Lückli 2470m

In the morning J D, who had been walking with us since Menton announced that blisters round his right ankle joints had become infected. He had damaged these joints many years before and as he was soon being reviewed for possible restorative surgery he decided to return to England.

With sadness we said our goodbyes at the bus stop in Vella and started the longest day's walk of this phase of our Alps traverse. From Vella we followed the road to Cumbel. Both of these large villages have many fine old alpine buildings. There is then a long descent to the river Glogn on paths, tracks and lanes. Not far above the river we went through the sleepy hamlet of Pleiv with its beautiful dark-brown weathered timber houses.

The bridge over the Glogn is some 1600m below our high point of the day. We turned left onto the main valley road and some way north of the bridge took the road to Duvin on the right. After a hairpin bend a path with red and white waymarks heads uphill to the right. The bottom sections of this path through woods are well-graded, but higher up it becomes much steeper and is somewhat exposed as it makes its way up the lip of a gorge. After this short tricky section the path crosses a meadow and rejoins the road just below Duvin. This hamlet has fine timber houses and we rested by the trough outside the church (above).

Although the steepest part of the first climb was over we faced a further 1300m ascent to the Güner Lückli. At first this is on a track through forest and then on a path that winds round the folds of the grassy cirque below the col. From the pass we could see Vella far below to the north and in the west the snow-capped hills that we had walked through on the previous days stretched to the horizon.

The way to Safien Plaz, 1155m below, begins on a comfortably-inclined path across high cow pasture. About halfway down we reached a cluster of old wooden chalets marked as the Zalöner Hütta on the map. From there a zigzagging track leads more steeply down through fir forest to a road. The final section is mainly on paths that short-cut the loops in this road as it winds down to Safien Plaz. At the base of the valley we stopped for a rest and a large glass of apfelsaft at an inn next to a reservoir full with strikingly blue water. This refreshment was very welcome as the last climb of the day starts on a long steep path that has been cut into the face of a cliff. Eventually the incline eases where the path enters forest and then comes out onto spectacularly flowered meadows, where there were magnificent views back to the Güner Lückli (above). At 1819m we reached the hamlet of Inner Glas.

The incline then eases and a gently-rising lane leads to the Berggasthaus Beverin www.berggasthaus-beverin.com.

This splendid old mountain inn at Usser Glas provided us with a comfortable bunk room with a shower that had "disco lights" and endless hot water. Dinner and breakfast were excellent. Andrew was due to leave us the next day, and catch a train from Thusis at 12.36. We were told it was a 4h30 walk to Thusis from Glasspass so we were relieved that the guesthouse agreed to give us breakfast at 07.00 to give him enough time to make this connection.

Day 52: Glaspass via Thusis to Obermutten (1836m)
20.1km, ascent 1390m, descent 1396m, 7h45
High point 1936m on the Muttner Höhi

Andrew and I set off at 07.30 at a brisk pace. Paradoxically the footpath to Thusis starts by going uphill. At the top of this ascent the path splits into three and none of these had signposts or waymarks. We selected the middle path, which turned out to be correct and after a while came to a boggy cow pasture with a sign indicating the way to Thusis. We followed red and white waymarks to the south, but unbeknown to us there are two waymarked paths leading from this pasture. We foolishly assumed that those starting at the southern corner of the marsh were signing the path to Thusis and followed these. The path turned disconcertingly to the southwest and then came to a distinctly dodgy "slag-heap" canyon, which we crossed with difficulty. On the far side was a signpost indicating a place not on our map and not mentioning Thusis. We got out the maps and compass and realized we must have taken the wrong route. The canyon was reversed and I suggested we follow the compass northwards, which should take us directly to the correct path. This was fine in principle, but we found ourselves pushing our way through a trackless fir plantation. It was tough going threading ourselves between dead branches in the darkness below the canopy. Eventually, we came out onto an alp and on the far side of this found an indistinct path running east along the edge of a canyon. We followed this downhill without much confidence that it was the right path. A few minutes later reassurance came from a clear signpost indicating the way to Thusis on the Walserweg.

Now the path became much better. We could start to make rapid progress, but it was already 09.15. After another 20 minutes in acceleration mode we joined a track and saw the remaining two Johns ahead of us. Their later start with careful progress clearly showed the benefits of a *festina lente* approach. Fortunately the route after this was straightforward and our haste in the end even enabled Andrew to get the earlier train at 11.38. The panic was over.

The afternoon's walk was no less exciting, but because of the nature of the route rather than poor navigation. After we had left JS and JM behind they had stopped for a leisurely lunch in Thusis and were consequently rather late getting to Obermutten. The Walserweg waymarks led me through the north-eastern suburbs of Thusis, across the Hinterrhein by a long suspension footbridge and through a tunnel under the main road to Chur. The Walserweg heads eastwards through Sils and then goes to the southwest before looping back in the opposite direction over the Carschenna Alp. I chose to shortcut this tortuous route by taking a path signposted at the east end of Sils to Obermutten on the Veia Surmirana. This veia is not mentioned on the SwissMap web site, but it more or less follows the route we had planned from Thusis to the Engiadin. It is labelled on the ground and described at www.wandersite.ch/Surmirana.html. This route climbs east to the Sils railway halt and then continues on the far side of the lines to a forest track above Campi. Some care with map reading is required to end up at the east end of the Carschenna Alp. From there a steeper track heads west-south-west to a clearing where there is a grotesque wood carving of a face.

To the left of this clearing red and white waymarks indicate a dubious path that heads steeply up through the woods. After a while the path becomes clearer, but the way much steeper. It is a long tough ascent in short zigzags. Shrubs and trees on the hillside are the only features that stop this being a distinctly scary route. Eventually the path levels off and winds round the top of a cliff before reaching a small but beautiful alp known as Crocs. There is a wooden chalet and a barn at the back of the alp, while 50 yards away across the meadow a cliff falls 500m to the larger alp at Carschenna. The climb is not over, for after

Crocs the path continues to climb steeply gaining a further 200m. Finally the path levels off and traverses across a steep meadow high above the valley of the Rein Posteriur (Hinterrhein) and gradually loses a little height before linking with a track that heads up a large floral alp (opposite) to the east. On reaching the top of this alp Obermutten comes into view lying in a hollow on the far side. The ancient wooden houses and church of the village are charming (above). We had reserved half-board accommodation in two twin rooms at the Gasthaus Post www.gasthauspost.ch/, a comfortable and attractive stopover.

Day 53: Obermutten to Savognin (1159)
19.7km, ascent 561m, descent 1257m, 5h30
High point the Plang Tarscholas 2133m

The path from Obermutten gradually climbs as it traverses to the southeast across a large cattle pasture. It was a beautiful day and a gentle cooling breeze added to the joy of the ascent. From the highpoint there was a fine view back to Obermutten in the north-west. Far below we could see the valley leading to Davos winding away to northeast. There followed a gradual descent through cow pasture, with the clanging of bovine bells.

On rounding a spur we entered the Sursés, which is the valley of the river Gelgia. This has many agricultural communities and judging by their buildings these villages and small towns have all been there for a long time. The route finding down to the valley floor is not easy, for the signposting and waymarking are erratic and attention has to be paid to the map and compass. On arriving in the small town Salouf we could see in the distance our destination - Savognin and the intermediate town - Riom. The route is not direct and there is a diversion uphill on a road to avoid a deep gorge. Just before Parsonz the road crosses the head of the gorge on a wooden bridge, after which we took a path that descends eastwards through the fields to Riom. The waymarked route crosses this town and then continues diagonally down past a castle through fields to a footbridge that spans the Gelgia (below). On the far side of this river a path leads past the east side of a lake to the modern Cube Hotel. It was a hot day and the lakeside was crowded with swimmers and sun-worshippers.

After a delay due to some confusion about our booking we were given a comfortable 4 bunk room that was accessed by ramps rather than stairs. This design allows guests to take their mountain bikes to the lobby of their room! We had plenty to eat at the buffet dinner and breakfast and overall the cost of the accommodation was comparatively low. The Cube www.cube-hotels.com/en is probably the best stopover in Savognin for walkers. We wandered into the town in the evening to inspect other hotels and restaurants. They did not seem very exciting.

Day 54: Savognin to Bivio (1769m)
21km, ascent 1400m, descent 840m, 7h25
High point the ponds at Tigias 1975m

The road up the valley links, via the Güglia pass, to the Engiadin. It attracts a steady stream of cars and commercial traffic. Fortunately the path we walked contours high on the eastern flank of the valley where the traffic was out of sight and inaudible. Bivio lies below the Güglia and Septimer passes and is at the crossroads of three languages and cultures. The diversity of language means that there are several versions of each place name and the signposting seems to use these randomly. Nevertheless, the name Veia Surmirana for the regional footpath we were now following is used throughout.

We started out from the Cube following a path on the northeast bank of the river and then headed straight up through the older parts of Savognin. This is a much more pleasant traverse of the small town than the busy main road with its rather drab shops and hotels. At the top edge of the town we joined a footpath that contours through woods along the north side of the valley. After passing above Tinizong the path starts to climb steeply up the left flank of a side valley, the Val Mulegna, until it joins a narrow road. We followed this road to the apex of a hairpin bend where we turned right onto a track that leads down to the Mulegna torrent and crosses this below an impressive waterfall. The track leads gradually down to a cluster of buildings at Plaz Beischen, where there was a fine new bench. JS admired this and thought of constructing a copy, while the rest of us sat on it and enjoyed the view back down the valley. From the bench we continued on the track, but took advantage of a shortcutting path between its zigzags. At Alp Sugen we passed a mobile milking parlour just before the track ends and then followed an undulating path to the delightful Alp Digl Plaz with its grazing cattle. A further climb on a rough path led to the high point of the day with a bench where we ate our sandwiches. The path then passes a couple of ponds (below) before descending to the large Alp Flix. The surrounding hills and flower-filled meadows make this an attractive place, but a road up to this alp services a number of rather untidy clusters of houses dotted across the meadowland. From the far end of Alp Flix there is a pleasant descent by a stream into forest. The path then traverses through marshy clearings, with drifts of dark mauve Bog Orchids, before undulating above the large dammed lake – the Lai da Marmorera. On this section JM engaged in conversation with a comely French-speaking Swiss walker who had caught up with him, but to his dismay as he reached where I was sitting on a bench above the hidden village of Marmorera she skipped away downhill. The final section of this walk climbs once again, rounding a large grassy cwm to

the Alp Natons. Here it started to rain gently. This fortunately did not amount to much and we were not too wet when we completed the final descent through woods to Bivio.

This is a pretty village with some fine buildings. Although it is set in beautiful alpine scenery it suffers, or perhaps in commercial terms benefits from, the busy main road. Tour buses and lorries queue to squeeze, one at a time, through the chicane formed by the old buildings in the centre of the village.

Our lodging – the Hotel Guidon www.hotel-guidon.ch/ is situated to the left of the main road on the way into Bivio. It was built about 50 years ago and has been run by the same family ever since. This rectangular box is no architectural gem. On the other hand we were made welcome, the food was good and the bedrooms were comfortable.

Day 55: Bivio to Surlej (1860m)
17km, ascent 700m, descent 606m, 5h00
High point the Pass dal Güglia 2284m

We had hoped to walk over the Septimerpass and Pass Lunghin on the way to Surlej, but it started to rain as we set out and the clouds were down to about 2400m. In the circumstances we decided to continue on the Veia Surmirana over the Pass dal Güglia. The disadvantage of this route is the busy main road that shares the same valley. The first section of the path has received a considerable amount of maintenance and was a pleasure to follow as it wound through woodland to the right of the road. After the farm at Capulota the going was considerably more dubious and it seems that few people walk this way. The route to the pass has several false summits before the col. This is on the watershed between the Rhine and the Danube and as we walked plenty of water was being shed. There were a couple of hopefuls trying to sell local products of the Grisons from a stall at the pass, but like the cars we hurried past in the rain. The descent was equally unused, but the waymarking was still good, guiding us down the hillside to the right of the road. Eventually, where there were some road works, the path crosses the road and then climbs to a ridge, which was hidden in the mist. It then descends once more to the road and on the far side crosses a stream. An excellent track then leads to a well-graded path that zigzags down to the Val Engiadin (non-locals call this Engadine) and the town of Sylvaplana.

As we descended the clouds miraculously parted, the sun came out and the lake turned from near-black to blue. We walked through the busy streets of Sylvaplana and then turned down towards the narrows in the lake where a bridge leads to Surlej. This expanded village exudes affluence. There only seem to be expensive houses and smart low-rise apartment blocks that are separated by immaculately tended gardens.

The quality of the service in our hotel there in no way matched its price so its name will not be mentioned. Happily we escaped from this pretentious place for our meals to a pleasant and more down-to-earth hotel/restaurant – the Süsom Surlej– near the base of the cable car. They gave us a good light lunch and later an excellent dinner. We should have booked rooms there www.nigglis.com. During the evening there was a violent thunderstorm as we ate our dinner. The outlook for the following day's walk at that point seemed bleak.

Day 56: Surlej to Pontresina (1805m)
18.6km, ascent 967m, descent 1021m, 6h15
High point the Fuorcla Surlej 2755m

Our pessimism was unfounded and the overnight rain had stopped by the time we escaped from our expensive hotel. As we walked up the track through pleasant woods towards the Fuorcla Surlej the weather progressively improved. By 2200m we were above the woods and zigzagging up an alp that must provide excellent skiing in the winter. There were fine views down to the valley with its two large lakes. Beyond the western lake we could see the route we had hoped to walk the previous day. Eventually we left the track for a waymarked path that leads to the intermediate cable car station at Murtel (2699m). This drab and massive place is on a north-facing slope at a height where there is little chance of plant life recovering from the building and ski run construction. Consequently in the summer the landscape around the station is pretty bleak. From here it is an easy traverse on a jeep track to Fuorcla Surlej.

Beside the mountain hut at the col a small lake cradled in the rock provides foreground for a splendid view of the 4049m Piz Bernina and its neighbours (opposite). We took the opportunity to have some apfelsaft in the hut. One of the warden's two English setter dogs was recovering from injuries sustained in an altercation with a marmot! So it seems marmots can do more than make deafening whistles.

The vegetation on the southern side of the col is a lot healthier than that met during the later stages of our ascent. This together with the view of the Bernina range and the absence of ski lifts made it a very pleasant descent in the warm sunshine on a well graded path. Where this path reaches the floor of the Val Roseg there is a hotel. Trips here by horse-drawn carriage and bicycle seem very popular, for motor traffic happily is excluded from the valley. After passing the hotel we crossed the Ova da Roseg, which is a substantial fast-flowing river fed by the summer melt from the large glaciers at the head of the valley. On the far side we reached a walking track that is closed to cyclists and horses. This gave us a pleasant riverside trek through the woods to Pontresina. On reaching the road it started to rain, but we just managed to scurry into the Sporthotel without getting soaked. We were given a warm welcome and had splendid rooms in this grand hotel: www.sporthotel.ch. The evening was spent eating our way through a substantial beuf bourguignon. An enthusiastic Tyrolean trio played in the restaurant; the antidote to this was copious Swiss pinot noir wine that gradually dulled our senses. It was a good end to a great walk across the quieter hills of Switzerland.

Days 56-71, Pontresina to Niederdorf

5 CHAPTER
DAYS 57-71 PONTRESINA TO NIEDERDORF
Across the Südtyrol from west to east

A logical way to walk from Pontresina to the most eastern point in Switzerland is to head east into the "no man's land" of Livigno. Officially this is part of Italy, but atypically for a valley south of the Italian Swiss border its river drains northwards from "Italy" into the Inn and then the Danube rather than south to the Po. It is also a tax free zone with border guards on the road-link to the rest of Italy. From Livigno we climbed into the northeast corner of the Lombardy province of Italy and the following day continued along the Italian-Swiss border to the Stilfser Joch. There Switzerland ends and we crossed into the Südtyrol. The western half of this German-speaking province of Italy is dominated by the Ortler Range, which rises to more than 3900m. Here the crossing of the Madritschjoch at 3124m was the highest point of our Alps traverse. This altitude provides a good reason for walking through the Südtyrol in early September rather than in June when snow might be a problem.

    The hills and valleys west of the Ortler have great beauty and some challenging sections. These led to the fertile Alto Adige valley where the apple orchards were heavy with ripe fruit. During the following 2 days we crossed more gentle hills before descending to the River Eisack, a tributary of the Adige. From there we climbed into the Dolomites and walked among these magnificent hills to their north-eastern corner at Niederdorf near the Austrian Border.

Day 57: Pontresina (1820m) to Livigno (1864m)
27km, up 700m, down 656m, 7h00
High point La Stretta 2476m

It is a long walk to Livigno, but the height gain and upward gradient are relatively modest. By contrast the initial descent from the border col at La Stretta is distinctly steep and we were glad this path was dry.

From the hotel we took the road towards the Surovas Station on the Bernina mountain railway. This crosses over the river and the busy road up the Val Bernina. We then took a cycle track that heads southeast between the railway and the river. After passing a bridge we followed a path that crosses the railway and winds through the forest above the tracks. There were wisps of mist around us as we walked through the pine woods, but the sky above was clear (below). Several squirrels, some red and others black scurried up pine trees as we passed. Where the path reaches the station at Morteratsch we could see the tips of the snow-clad peaks of the Piz Bernina range. On the other side of the level crossing we passed a hotel and then took a path to the right climbing in zigzags through pine woods. At the top of the woods a short descent led to open pasture. The enjoyment of this meadow-land was tempered by the noise from the busy valley road not far to our left. After passing the Bernina Suot railway station we could see, on the far side of the railway and main road, the gravel track that winds up the Val da Fain. We followed this track to a bridge over the river and then on into the tranquillity and beauty of this unspoilt side valley. There were ever-increasing views back to the white ridges of Piz Bernina and its satellite peaks set against the cloudless blue sky (below). The track ends at the Alp da Stretta farmhouse. Here the delicious apple-strudel freshly-baked by the farmer's wife should not be missed. After the farm the path to the Italian border is relatively level and passes a series of pools that give beautiful reflections of the hills ahead.

From the Stretta pass there is a distinctly steep descent of some 400m to the busy valley road. This requires some care, but was not dangerous in the dry. Walking down the road after this descent was a greater hazard. A racing van, followed so closely by a car that the driver could see nothing but the van ahead both overtook a car and drove an oncoming motorcyclist off the road. Fortunately it was one of the few places where a motorcyclist could pull off the road. Soon after this we were glad to be able to follow a pleasant vehicle-free track to the right of the road. This eventually crosses the main road near a bridge and then passes a number of buildings before crossing a new bridge to the left that leads to a paved cycle/pedestrian track. This pleasant track goes to the southern edge of Livigno where we joined the main road and continued on this to the Sporting Hotel. This old style chalet building http://sporting.bormolinihotels.com was bedecked with a mass of flowers. We were given a twin-bedded room and our evening meal was taken in the hotel's restaurant. I greedily ordered porcini as a starter as well as with a steak for the next course. These delicious fungal treats are a distinct advantage of walking in Northern Italy in the autumn.

Day 58: Livigno to La Brocchetta (1884m)
24.0km, up 594m, down 504m, 6h30
High point the Passo de Valle Alpisella 2284m

We headed north down the road from the hotel towards the centre of Livigno where JS bought a yellow baseball cap with embroidery celebrating the French football team's world cup victory at the end of the last century. The shopkeeper was clearly delighted to be shifting this historic stock. Livigno has developed as a strip along the main road, but

the houses are traditional in style and the green well-grassed ski hills rising on either side make this a pleasant enough walk. At the end of the town we crossed the river and followed a track on its east bank, soon reaching the point where the river flows into the Lago di Livigno. Here there were stunning reflections of the steep hills on the far side of this lake. We crossed the bridge at the mouth of the Canale Torto and then followed a well-made and broad track to the right that climbs to the southeast. After a while the track levels off and traverses high above the canale. It then enters the Val Alpisella and crosses the valley stream on a narrow wooden bridge. On the far side of the bridge the track was being much used by mountain bikers. It climbs steeply up the southern side of the valley in two long zigzags to a small lake near the Passo de Valle Alpisella (above). From there we had fine views onwards to the snowy peaks of the high Ortler range. These peaks would dominate the views for the next 3 days. A short way after the pass we walked onto the alp and rested in the warm midday sun on the grass eating sandwiches and enjoying the fine views of the sharp rocky ridges on either side of the valley. There followed a pleasant gradual descent to the south west corner of the Lago di San Giacomo di Fraéle, from where a dirt road runs along its southern shore. We followed this road past the dam that separates this upper lake from the lower Lago di Cancano.

Our lodging for the night, the Ristoro/Refugio Monte Scale www.cancano.com, lies at the east end of the second lake well above the massive curved barrage. We had a twin bedroom with a shower. The evening meal and breakfast were unpretentious, but satisfying. The Monte Scale is convenient for this walk, welcoming and a pleasant economical place to stay.

Day 59: La Brocchetta to Trafoi (1543)
23.5km, up 1303m, down 1626m, 7h45
High point the Drei-Sprachen-Spitz 2853m

The route on this deceptively long day stays near the line of the Italian/Swiss border until the Stilfser Joch at the east end of Switzerland, where we entered the German-speaking Südtyrol province of Italy.

After crossing the vertiginously high barrage that lies below the Monte Scale Refuge we climbed on a rough road past a church before descending through forest to gain access to the Valle Forcola. The track entering this valley is cut into its steep rocky west wall (below). It then climbs to the farmstead at Baita di Forcola. Beyond is a long zigzag that leads to the top of a rock band. The track then winds upwards through pleasant meadows to 2544m were it enters the grassy upper valley. There is a slight descent from here before the inevitable climb up the gravelly head wall to the Brocchetta di Forcola at 2768m. On the approach to the col there are views back to the Bernina range. Beyond lies a wide grassy valley that rises to the Stilfser Joch, with its cluster of commercial buildings. From there, beyond of the deep Trafoi valley, the snow-capped Ortler massive rises to 3901m (below).

Soon after leaving the peace of the Forcola Valley we started to hear a constant stream of revving motorcycles, racing up the road from Bormio to the Stilfsler Joch as we traversed to the left from the brocchetta. The path gradually descends to the Pass Umbrail (2581m). For most of this route the path is good, but there are one or two marginally delicate sections where it crosses gullies. The way from the Pass Umbrail on foot follows a path that climbs well to the north of the road on the Swiss side of the border. This rises in zigzags to the ridge that runs north from the Drei-Sprachen-Spitz (Three-Language-Peak), for this summit lies at the junction of Switzerland, Lombardy and the Südtyrol. There is a good path along the ridge southwards to the Stilfser Joch. We had planned to go north along the Drei-Sprachen-Spitz ridge, before descending to Trafoi, but this is shown as a difficult route on the map and it looked it. As we had already had a tough day and the descent to Trafoi by any route is long and steep we decided to take the line of least resistance via the Stifsler Joch. The crowds at this pass, together with the noise, smell of motorbike fumes and fast food, make it no place to linger. We quickly made our way through the throng at the pass and walked down the road through 12 hairpin bends to a point about 250m below the col. From there we walked down the grassy valley below and to the right of the road (below). This leads to the Hotel Franzenshöhe (2189m), which lies at the mouth of the hanging

valley seen in the photo. Footpath 13 descends eastwards from the hotel through quiet, attractive woodland, where we got glimpses up to the north ridge of the Ortler, which we were to cross the following day. At about 1700m we joined footpath 10 and headed north through the forest on a gradual descent to Trafoi. After joining a lane at the entrance to the village there is a right fork to a gate, beyond which the route crosses a meadow to the church. The path then leads down past a nature centre to the Bella Vista hotel www.bella-vista.it. This period 3 star hotel has been completely modernised. True to its name the Bella Vista has fine views southwards to the Ortler through the massive picture windows of the dining room. The hotel is run by the Thöni family; Gustav Thöni, a native of Trafoi, is a former Olympic and World Cup ski champion. Andrew joined us at the Bella Vista and we were given a comfortable triple room. The food was excellent and the service efficient and welcoming. Away from the main road, the forest and mountain scenery around Trafoi are exceptionally beautiful.

Day 60: Trafoi to Coston Sulden (1973m)
16.0km, up 1168m, down 987m, 6h15
High point on the Ortler's north ridge 2341m

Paths in the Südtyrol are numbered and these numbers appear both on signposts as well as being written in black on the white section of many of the red and white waymarks. This system generally works well, but becomes confusing when the numbers on the maps do not match those on the ground.

Our route followed path 19. The actual start of this path differed a little from that shown on the map. A signpost on the right side of the forecourt of the hotel indicates a path, labelled 19. This leads in zigzags down to the river. We followed this path and then headed downstream along the left bank to a wooden bridge. On the far side there is a long steep climb through forest, still on 19. Shortly after passing the ruins of the Alpenrose hut the path splits and we followed the left fork labelled 19B. This skirts round a number of steep gullies (below) before reaching easier ground at the beautifully sited Obere Schäferhütte. This small hut is obviously in use, presumably by a shepherd, although no one was at home when we passed.

From the hut the path descends slightly to a junction, where we took the right fork on a path labelled 26 on the waymarks, but 22A on the map. There are great views from this path, which traverses over the north ridge of the Ortler reaching a high point of 2341m (below). On the far side of the ridge we came to a small white chapel – the St Wendelin Kapelle. Beyond this are the ruins of a manganese mine, which was presumably associated with the chapel and the now-abandoned adjacent buildings. There is no easy way down from here, so the ore from the mine must have been taken to the valley by a cable lift, but there are no signs of this now.

From the chapel footpath 26 heads steeply down past the abandoned buildings where we disturbed sheep that were using these to shelter from the midday sun. The path leads in zigzags down a long, consistently steep, but safe descent to the river in the Sulden Valley. The waymarking is good throughout. On arriving at the river we discovered the bridge that used to carry 26/22A to the houses at Aussersulden had been swept away. There was a lot of water cascading down this substantial river and we judged that an attempt at a crossing would be dangerous. The map suggests there might be an unclassified footpath heading south and we found this leading off from 26 a little above the river. This path climbs through forest to a steep meadow where it becomes indistinct. Fortunately, there is a continuation heading into more woods about halfway up the far side of the meadow. This path soon reaches a gravelly river gorge which we crossed. On the far side a well-made forestry track led us to the main valley road. We then headed up the road climbing through four right-angled bends before the road levelled off and continued through fields that were carpeted with autumn crocuses. On entering Sulden a right fork led to footpath 7. This heads south above the west bank of the river Solda on a broad and well made path. Eventually we came to a bridge which joins a road that leads to the bottom Coston Sulden cable car station. We walked past the two hotels to the east of the station and then headed down on a road to the village of Coston Sulden. Pensione Eden www.pension-eden.com lies at the end of the first turning to the left in the village. We were given a double and single room and the meals in this comfortable and popular pension were excellent.

Day 61: Coston Sulden to St Maria in der Schmelz (1538m)
23.1km, up 1333m, down 1732m, 7h50
High point the Madritschjoch 3124m

On this long walk we crossed the Madritschjoch, the highest point on our entire Alps traverse. The route presented no problems in the good conditions that prevailed on our walk. The suggestion of technical difficulty indicated by the dots rather than dashes marking this footpath on the map can only reflect the altitude.

The walk starts on the pleasant 2A footpath climbing through scrub to the left of the first section of the cable car. Just before the middle lift station the path briefly joins a rough ski-station service track. There is then a section on a path that climbs above the track before rejoining it where it winds onto a lateral moraine. The track then curves round a rock promontory on its way to the top cable car station. The pink-painted Schaubachhütte (2581m) is spectacularly-placed below this station with views across the massive gravel-covered glacier to the east face of the Ortler (opposite).

Crowds were spilling out of the top cable car station as we passed and consequently the next section of our walk to the Madritschhütte (2818m) was somewhat busy. Many from the crowd succumbed to the temptation of refreshment at this hut so there was less of a throng as we made our way up the final 300m to the Madritschjoch (3124m). The hillside here is composed of grey fractured-slate gravel and although there were snowfields on either side of the path our route remained free of snow. From the col there is a fine view forward down the Madritschtal, which after the first two or three hundred meters was green, in contrast to the grey of the valley we were leaving. The south side of the Madritschtal rises to a large white glacier field below an east west ridge of hills that clearly have more stable rock than those in the Ortler range. The first section of yellow stony path on this side of the col was quite steep but not difficult. Soon we reached a relatively flat alp, where we rested for a while before descending steeply again to another flat alpine meadow. At the west end of this meadow we could see the Zufallhütte to our right perched on a small plateau on the top of a rocky outcrop (above). We followed the 151 path where this descends to the left just before the outcrop. On reaching a track running across another relatively flat meadow we turned right towards the base of the Zufallhütte outcrop. Just before this rock we turned left onto footpath 36, a quiet footpath that runs down the length of the Martelltal on its south-east flank. This beautiful and tranquil route down the valley has spectacular views of falls in the river (opposite). The 36 runs along the south shore of the Zurfritsee as a track, but before and after this lake it is an exhausting, but enchanting path with many roots and rocks to negotiate as well as plenty of up and down. By the time we reached the Hotel Waldheim just after the chapel of St Maria in der Schmelz, we knew we had had a good day's walk. This pleasant and welcoming 3 star Hotel/Restaurant www.waldheim.info provided good accommodation in a 3 bed room and excellent meals.

Day 62: St Maria in der Schmelz to St Gertrude (1484m)
15.7km, up 1440m, down 1516m, 7h30
High point col south of the Soyscharte 2887m

There seems to be no easy way to cross from the Martelltal to the upper Ultnertal. The routes over all three of the passes are marked on the map in red dots indicating that these are difficult passes and local intelligence confirms this. In addition when we woke it was apparent that the fine weather had deserted us and the forecast for heavy rain with snow above 2500m turned out to be accurate. These factors led John and me to decide to walk for an hour down to the village of Grand and from there get a bus into the Alto Adige valley. There we hoped to get a train to Lana and then a bus up the Ultnertal to St Gertraud.

Andrew said that he fancied facing the weather and the steep high pass. He continued on footpath 36 to Hölderle where he picked up footpath 4. This took him to the east uphill passing an alpine pasture hut at Soyalm (2071 m). As the path approaches the Soyscharte it apparently becomes distinctly steep and ascends on unstable scree. It seems that this section was not easy going in the wet snow storm and there was much skidding. Andrew reckoned we would not have enjoyed this part of his route. From the col the path, now named 141, descends south-eastwards on somewhat easier ground to another alpine pasture hut, the Ausser Pilsberg Alm. It then continues in the same general direction to the village of St Gertraud, where we had booked a triple room at the 3 star Hotel Ultnerhoff. They claimed we had cancelled our booking, which we had not, but this was not serious, for they did have a room for us and, importantly, a good drying room.

The old men managed to walk to Grand before the heavy rain started. We were pleased to find that from there a bus runs to the banhoff at Goldring, at least once an hour during the day. We got a bus after waiting only 10 minutes and a train to Meran arrived 3 minutes after we reached the station. The train was as crowded as the London tube in rush-hour, but it got us safely to Meran, where we boarded a train on the adjacent platform that took us to the next stop – Lana Postal. From there frequent busses go to central Lana, but this is not clear, for they carry a label indicating their final destination – the banhoff at Meran. Consequently we walked into Lana where it started to rain heavily. We sought refuge in a cafe, where we each had a toasted

baguette and coffee. This cheered us up, but eventually we had to make a move. After putting on our waterproof gear we set off for the bus station to see if we could get transport up the Ultnertal. We eventually found the right place to catch a suitable bus. This is at the roundabout at the base of the road up the Ultnertal rather than the bus station. Fortunately we only had to wait 15 minutes for a bus that would take us to St Gertraud. The bus was almost full with senior-school pupils who were returning to their homes in the Ultnertal. We found the last two seats and sat with our dripping rucksacks on our knees. After the village of St Pankraz, where several people got off, we were able to spread out a little. It was still raining heavily when we reached St Gertraud, where we followed the signs to our hotel. This lies at the far end of the village.

Andrew had already arrived. Despite the booking confusion the Ultnerhoff was an excellent stopover www.ultnerhof.com/. This was the only hotel where we had failed to get booking confirmation in writing or email. The booking had been accepted by telephone, albeit with assurances that there would be no problem with the reservation.

Day 63: St Gertrude to St Walburg (1424m)
19.0km, up 974m, down 1342m, 6h20
High point the Kaserfeld Alm 1945m

The rain had passed by the morning and the hills at the head of the valley were peppered with new snow. We walked past the village church (below) and followed the valley road for a couple of hundred meters or so before turning left onto the clearly signed footpath 143. This well-made path climbs steeply through woods and gives glimpses back to

the village. At a splitting of the ways we took the lower fork and this took us up to the high point of the day, an alpine pasture hut – the Kaserfeld Alm (1945m). Here we sat in the warm sunshine and enjoyed cups of coffee in the company of two recumbent sows, who also appeared to be enjoying the sun (opposite). From this pasture hut most of the rest of the walk to St Walberg is a gradual descent through alp and woodland. Successively we walked on footpaths 14, 14B and 12 before reaching the hamlet of Inergrub, where we joined a mountain road and continued to the church at St Moritz. From there track 11 descends from below the east end of the church and after a while leaves the track for a green path on the right. This falls steeply to a road, where we turned right crossing a bridge before taking a left fork to buildings at Moos. Once past these the 11 again becomes a pleasant grassy track that eventually joins a lane. We followed this lane ignoring two forks to the left, but at a third fork took the left branch going uphill. At a hairpin our route turned right onto a track named the Sunnenseitnweg. This climbs round a rocky gorge and then descends to a lane near the Obereggen farm. We turned east down this lane that leads to the main valley road in St Walberg. The Gasthoff Eggwirt is 100m or so up the main road to the right www.eggwirt.it. This delightful late 19th century hotel has conserved many of its original features, particularly in the dining rooms. The bedrooms have been modified to provide modern comforts.

Day 64: St Walburg to Lana (274m)
20.0km, up 850m, down 1665m, 6h40
High point the Unterdurach 1280m

The first half of the walk, to St Pankraz, is on the Ultner Talweg. We thought that this would be a well-used and straightforward footpath. In reality it turns out to have some delicate sections, particularly as it approaches St Pankraz and was somewhat overgrown in places. Nevertheless, this is a beautiful and continually interesting route.

Footpath 5, which largely follows lanes on the alp above the Ultner Talweg, probably provides a more straightforward, but possibly less interesting way to reach St Pankraz.

The final section of the walk to Lana was also delightful in this season of mellow fruitfulness. From the east end of St Pankraz there is a short section along the main valley road to the start of footpath 6. Happily a pavement here protects walkers from the traffic on the busy road. Footpath 6 leaves the road to the right passing along the side of a field on the edge of a steep gorge. It then passes an apple orchard before zigzagging down on a safe path to the river. On the other side of a wooden bridge there is a long steep zigzagging climb out of the gorge. This good path through woods took us to a little-used lane some 400m above the river. We followed this lane downhill, at one stage passing through a tunnel. There was one shortcut after this before we came out of the forest and started to pass apple orchards. The crop was just about to be harvested and there was a marvellous smell of apples. Footpath 6 leaves the lane here and descends through further orchards (above) to the outskirts of Lana. The walk down through the orchards was a delightful end to the two wonderful days we had spent walking along the Ultnertal. Lana is the lowest point on our walk between Menton and Vittorio-Veneto and our stopover was the hotel Schwarzschmied www.schwarzschmied.com. This smart four star hotel was a pleasant place to mark Andrew's last night on the walk. The food was outstanding, but it is hardly a stopover where one would expect to meet backpackers.

Day 65: Lana to the Auener Hof (1613)
18.0km, up 1740m, down 401m, 7h00
High point the Auener Jöchl 1925 m

We reversed the walk we had done on our detour a few days earlier between Lana and the station at Lana Postal, but this time in brilliant sunshine. At the railway we said our goodbyes to Andrew, before continuing to the Via Roma in the village of Postal where we turned right. At the end of the village we turned left into a lane signposted the Graf Walkmar Weg. This short lane goes uphill looping to the right. From the end of the lane a footpath leads through woods to a path junction where there is a left turn onto a stone-paved track marked with red and white waymarks. This track is labelled as B on the map and signposted as the Sunseitnsteig. It is a pleasant but exhausting climb through the woods of the steep northern escarpment of the Alto Adige to a green alp some 670m above the valley. We passed under the cable car that links Postal with the village of Vöran, from where the green apple orchards on the valley floor formed a chequer board (below). The Sunseitnsteig then turns left onto a lane. This was followed for a short way before we moved onto a marked path that led upwards through woods and fields to Vöran. On the far side of the village the route heads eastwards on route 1, signposted to the Grüner Baum Inn. This route is mostly on road with some shortcuts. At the inn we joined a lane that heads uphill to the north. Footpath 16 runs beside this lane, at first through forest and then across vividly green alp. Eventually the lane loops round to the right and route 11 leaves to the left. Signposts point to the final turns to the Leaderalm. In the garden of this inn many people were enjoying a sunny "pub lunch", but as we were expecting a good meal in the evening we resisted the temptation to join them. Instead we continued east on 11 through forest climbing gradually. After a while the path joins a strada bianca briefly before continuing as

a path to the right of the strada. It then rejoins the strada and continues to a fork where the signs to the Auener Jöchl are followed to the right. Almost immediately the 11 becomes a path again to the right that eventually rejoins the strada bianca, which continues to climb gently through forest. At one point a clearing in the trees gives a fine view of the distant dolomite rock walls of the Rosengarten. Some half a km before reaching the Auener Jöchl the track comes out of the forest and climbs as a path to the elaborately-signposted broad col (above). After resting for a while on the bench under the signpost we started the descent on the wide path 2, past the mountain restaurant at the Auener Alm. Here there is a new strada bianca, which is not marked on the map. We joined this briefly before descending to the right on the marked rough track that leads to a road. At a hairpin bend we headed right to the Sarner Skihütte www.sarnerskihuette.com/. Our stopover was the four-star Hotel/Restaurant Auenerhof, which has a Michelin-starred restaurant www.auenerhof.it. It lies in a secluded sunny spot at the end of a short lane that runs round the back of the Sarner Skihütte Inn. Anne and Pam joined us here, arriving in a silver-painted VW Golf estate, which they had picked up at Munich airport. We had luxurious rooms and there was a panoramic view of the south-western Dolomites from the dining room (above). We enjoyed a long evening lingering over their 6 course tasting menu. Not surprisingly at 140€/person for dinner bed and breakfast this was our most expensive stop-over on the entire Alps Traverse, but everything about our stay at the Auenerhof approached perfection. We could only be happy with this memorable visit as a very occasional treat.

Day 66: Auener Hof to Villanders (1058m)
23.6km, up 1300m, down 1848m, 8h00
High point the Totenkirchl 2186m

This was the last day before the Dolomites and there were views of these massive rocky outcrops from the day's high point and during our descent to Villanders. We had a pleasant walk down to the large village of Sarnthein on footpath 2. To start with the path goes through forest, while nearer Sarnthein it crosses steep meadows before reaching the village. We passed on the right side of the church and then took a small lane over a bridge and up to the main road. On the far side of the road the footpath 3/18 goes up steps to a lane and then climbs on the side of a meadow. After some more steps we reached an impressively-sited castle. From there we followed a lane, signposted 6/18 that winds round to the north and after 0.7km becomes footpath 6, climbing steadily uphill as a track through the forest. After rising 200m the track turns to the south and goes round a steep grassy enclosure before meeting another track and continuing north above the meadow still as 6. This track climbs slowly to 1700m and stays at this height for some time, winding round to the east. Eventually 6 leaves the track to the right as a path and climbs through sparse pine forest to a newly-made forest road, which is not marked on the map. The footpath continues above the road to a col at (2083m).

The way ahead crosses an isolated valley with two lakes (above) before climbing to the high point of the day – the Totenkirchl. From this white-painted chapel the Dolomite outcrops could be picked out in the late afternoon sun. This magnificent panorama remained in view as we walked from the chapel ESE on a strada bianca across the grassy expanse of the Villanderer Alm. When we reached the Gasserhütte there were crowds at a massive road-head car park. Happily we were soon on our own again as we started to descend more steeply on footpath 7. This initially runs through woods along a narrow ski run with wooden protection boards on the outside of its bends. After crossing a road the path, now 10, becomes an ancient stone-paved track. This track has obviously been a much-used way up to the high alp in the past, for the stones have been grooved on either side by the passage of numerous cartwheels over many years (below). The long, pleasant descent on route 10 to the small town of Villanders happily only twice crosses the busy road leading to the Gasserhütte car park.

In Villanders we lodged in the hotel restaurant Ansatz zum Steinbock www.zumsteinbock.com. It is a large old building set near the church in a narrow street above the main road. The hotel has a maze of passages and staircases and has been sensitively modernized making it a very pleasant place to stay. The girls were waiting for us in a small walled garden at the entrance to the hotel, where we happily downed two large beers as they sipped cappuccinos.

Day 67: Villanders to Schutzhütte Raschötz (2170m)
18.2km, up 1800m, down 500m, 7h00
High point the Ausserraschöts 2202m

Across the road from the hotel we picked up footpath 4, which leads down to Klausen on paths and lanes. This was a delightful quiet descent in the morning sunshine away from the main road, past gardens and vineyards. Klausen lies in the valley where the busy autostrada takes a constant stream of traffic up to the Brenner Pass. Consequently it was a surprise to find that Klausen is a beautiful old town with fine houses, clustered together in narrow bustling and largely traffic free streets.

Thoughtfully the autostrada has been placed well above the town on the far side of the river and its traffic is almost inaudible in the streets. At the far end of a charming square we crossed a bridge over the river and climbed covered steps and then narrow lanes. These led us to a road that passes under the autostrada.

On the far side footpath 10 climbs steeply from the road though meadows and woods. When it reaches a lane at Moar zu Tassis the path turns to the north and traverses above a wood at the edge of fields. It descends a little before climbing to the buildings at Fonteklaus. From the apex of the first bend in the lane out of Fonteklaus a path climbs through a forested valley to a cluster of buildings at Zicker. We then followed a path that shortcuts the road zigzaging up to Figist. Here a

horizontal lane leads north-west to the Gasthoff at Gnoll. This looks like a pleasant place and has fine views across the valley. Route 7 heads up from there through the woods on a mixture of tracks and paths. At a junction where an alternative 7 climbs to a ridge we continued on the lower 7 that climbs through woodland to a foresters' hut at Tschatterlin. There is then a long horizontal traverse on a path marked on the map as 7/31A. The path now is waymarked with yellow rather than red and white paint marks, which led us to question whether we had strayed off 7. Thankfully the path eventually meets a broad ridge, where 7 is clearly signposted as a wide path leading up the Tschatterlin Sattel where the alternative 7 joins from the right.

From this grassy col a good path, largely paved with granite slabs, climbs 328m to the Ausserraschotz plateau. The climb gives ever more splendid views of the hills we had crossed the previous days (opposite). It was a fine afternoon and the series of blue ridges contrasted with the haze in the intervening valleys.

If these views were provocative nothing prepared us for the majestic massive rocky peaks of the Dolomites that jumped at us when we rounded the ridge and stepped onto the high plateau above Ortisie. It was a short walk across the plateau to our lodgings at the Schutzhütte Raschötz www.rifugiorasciesa.com. There we found Pam and Anne waiting for us. They had come up on the new mountain railway from Ortisei, with its top station 1.4km east of the hut. We have stayed in many huts since we left Menton, but have never before found one with rooms with fine linen on double beds and a private bathrooms. That explains why the accommodation fees were about twice that of the average hut. As we sipped beers on the terrace of the hut at 2100m the sun set slowly on the extraordinary hills (above). It was an exceptional evening. The food was ample, but the girls were not too keen on the huge dumplings served with goulash. On the other hand they had not walked up from Klausen.

Day 68: Schutzhütte Raschötz to Seres (1614m)
20.5km, up 797m, down 1412m, 6h20
High point the Kreuzjoch 2299m

John and I said our goodbyes and set off in brilliant sunshine and cool refreshing air. This was long before the mountain railway released its first passengers of the day onto the high alp, so we were alone during the hour it took us to reach the Brogelshütte. From there we descended into a lightly wooded valley to start our long walk below the massive cliffs of the Geisler Odel. It remained quiet until we had passed the

path that zigzags up steeply to the Mitagsschart. It is possible to pass between the highest rock pillars of the Odel range via this path, but our route continued below the cliffs. It was about noon when we first encountered people walking to the west on a circuit from the car park at the Zanser Alm. For mid week in September it was extraordinary; we must have passed hundreds of people on the path over the next hour. This even makes the popular routes in the English Lake District at half term seem quiet, which they are not. As quickly as the crowds had come they vanished, when we left this popular circuit and began the long steep climb to the Kreuzjoch. From the joch there were memorable views back to the Odel (above). It seemed impossible that the magnificence of the mountain scenery we had enjoyed in the previous 2 days could continue, but the views ahead from the col were equally stunning and stretched onwards as far as the eye could see. We were not going to have any anticlimaxes as we headed east to Niederdorf. Indeed this was the case all the way to Vittorio-Veneto.

The walk down the upper Val Lungi on footpath 5 in the late afternoon sunshine was special. The alp had been mowed and the hay gathered. Autumn crocuses poked through the immaculate grassland on either side of the strada bianca and the massive cliffs of the Piz Somplunt on our right were bathed in the evening sun. This is a quiet valley and no more than a couple of other walkers were seen during the hour or so it took to reach the road that leads to Seres and our hotel. We stayed at the Pension Odles www.odles.it. This unconventional Pension is built next to the family farm in a pretty location. The buildings are attractive with plenty of primitive art and memorabilia. We had comfortable rooms and the simple evening meal was satisfying and filling. The family that runs the hotel seems to do this on a part-time basis. We were left very much to our own devices in the modern hotel. The meals were served in a "restaurant" in an adjacent old wooden building.

Day 69: Seres to Guesthouse Ciurnadú Alta Badia (1614m)
19.6km, up 1123m, down 1107m, 6h30
High point the Heiligkreuz Santa Croce 2047m

This was the second wet day of this phase of the walk and only our fourth since leaving Menton. We put on our waterproof gear and set off down the road to the junction where we picked up the well-signed footpath 6. This led us up through forest to the Juel Sattel (1725m). There was then a moist descent on a strada bianca to the edge of village of Pescol, from where we walked down though meadow-land, still on footpath 6. The last section of the route to Badia is on a lane.

In the town we took the diagonal left from the busy main road that crosses a bridge to the quieter village of St Leonhard. Here, at the bottom of the humming express chair lift, we picked up footpath 7. This follows the general line of the chair lift to the Hospitz la Cruzs at 2047m. We stopped at a restaurant near the middle lift station for a coffee, but by the time we were ready to leave, the rain had changed from drizzle to downpour, but we pushed on. Dotted along the way to the hospitz are the Stations of the Cross that allowed us to monitor our progress. After sheltering briefly in the entrance to the hospitz church we set off in a northerly direction down footpath 15, crossing newly-mown alp. Footpath labelling at the start of 15 was unambiguous, but as we reached the south side of the Val de Fanes this was less clear, for the several different footpaths in this valley seem to be labelled either 15 or 13. Fortunately the visibility, despite the rain, was sufficient to allow us to navigate our way from the map round the valley to the north side where we found the Guesthouse Ciurnadú www.ciurnadu.it. We had time to shower and change into dry clothes before the girls found the lane that leads to this wonderfully-sited hotel. The rooms at the Ciurnadú are very comfortable and the restaurant excellent. Everything about this hotel is first class and very good value. It is well worth a return visit.

Day 70: Ciurnadú to Berggasthaus Pederü (1577m)
15.0km, up 1021m, down 1029m, 5h30
High point the Antoniusjoch 2468 m

After the rain of the previous day we woke to perfect weather and there was a dusting of snow on the Dolomite peaks across the valley. The walk took us up the Val de Fanes from the beautiful alp of the lower valley to magnificent mountain scenery at the Antoniusjoch (above).

First we retraced our steps to the head of the lower valley and took a strada bianca labelled on the map as the first of two footpaths 13, but on the ground it is neither signposted nor waymarked. After a while, by some wooden barns, the strada turns to the left and heads towards white cliffs to the north, but we needed to go eastwards. Consequently we abandoned the track and headed across marshy meadow until we found a grassy track. This soon joined the way-marked footpath 13, which we followed uphill. Gradually the forest thins and becomes scrubby before giving way to the Dolomite scree of the upper valley. The footpath can now be seen climbing high on the north side of the valley leading to the inevitable final zigzags before the col. The path turned out to provide an excellent and safe route up this wonderful cwm. There were extraordinary views back from the col of the immediate massive rock faces and the distant snow-clad hills (opposite). The way forward from the col was again on a path high on the north side of the valley, but now the scree was finer and mixed with yellow mud, which in places made our footing less sure. Where the scree reached the Plan des Sarens Alp some men were erecting a substantial wooden fence that would prevent cattle from plunging over the cliff to our left. We continued down grassy slopes with interspersed dolomite pavement before negotiating a series of natural rock terraces to reach the top end of a strada bianca by a stream that runs from the small lake near the Ucia Lavareia. As we walked down the strada mountain bikers were toiling upwards to this hut. After about a km a signpost indicates footpath 7 running to the left of the road. This provided a delightful and peaceful route down to our destination. Before the lip of a hanging valley the stream sinks into the dolomite and the face below forms a steep funnel of compressed fine scree with the stream emerging once again from its base. The excellent path zigzags spectacularly down this face (above) before reaching flat ground. From there we saw the girls

waving from the third-floor balcony on the large Berggasthaus Pederü www.pederue.it. On the terrace where we sipped our beers there was a crowd of excited French walkers engaged in lively conversation. Soon the sun sank below the high peaks to our right and the walkers made for their bus leaving us alone in the uncomfortably cooling mountain air. The rooms were pleasant, but the kitchen staff were rather too keen to get us to the dining room early for our supper so that they could go home.

Day 71: Berggasthaus Pederü to Niederdorf (1151m)
20.0km, up 904m, down 1250m, 6h00
High point the Seitenbachscharte 2331m

The final day of this stage of the walk was again sunny and we set off on an extraordinary road that climbs in short steep zigzags up a gully to the east of the Berggasthaus. This road gives access to a large plateau that must provide valuable summer grazing. After the road levels off we took path 7A to the left. This crosses a stream and climbs in two long zigzags through 2000m before reaching the Plan de Lasta. At the top of this climb there are stunning views of distant blue hills to the east, where we were to walk the following year. Our route, now on a track, heads round to the north leading to the rather grand Senneshütte. From there track 24 climbs gradually NE across high lonely alp, finally arriving at the northern escarpment of the plateau where rock faces plunge 1000m to the forests that surround Pragser Wildsee. The impressive rock jaws of the Seitenbachschart (2422m) provide access to the Sennesertal, one of the two weaknesses in the rock barrier where it is possible to scramble down the steep headwall of a cirque (opposite). It was good that the weather was fine for this tricky but enjoyable descent. We were alone in this immense cirque and saw no one until we had lost 900m. The broad pleasant alp at the bottom of the cliffs has a restaurant – the Grünwaldalm, which is frequented by folk enjoying a gentle walk from the car park at the foot of the Pragser Wildsee. We walked on to the shore of this beautiful lake (below), where we lingered for a while before continuing to the north end of the lake. There a hotel with car parks is a popular destination with plenty of visitors. As soon as we left the hotel we again found solitude on footpath 1 where it enters the forest below the lake. This well-made gravel path leads down through pleasant woodland to a point on the main road a few hundred meters above the pretty village of Schmieden. We turned into the village, following the quiet main street and continuing beyond through fields to the main road. Our hotel – the Edelweiss www.hoteledelweiss.info/en/ is a short distance north along this road. This comfortable hotel has an excellent restaurant and was a good place to spend the last evening of this phase of our traverse of the Alps.

Days 72-82, Niederdorf to Vittorio-Veneto

6 CHAPTER
DAYS 72-82 NIEDERDORF-VITTORIO-VENETO
North to South through the Eastern Dolomites

The final 11 days of our 82-day walk crossed the eastern dolomites from north to south. With the exception of the Drei Zinnen range these hills are less-visited than the western Dolomites, but their challenging rocky peaks provided some of the finest walking of our traverse of the Alps. This last section of our long walk proved to be every bit as enjoyable as the rest of our journey. The only regret is that there was not more of it, but there are always new challenges to come.

JD at the Forcla de Leone on Day 77

Day 72: Gasthof Edelweiss Niederdorf to Toblacher See (1263m)
17.6km, up 1157m, down 1116m, 6h30
High point the Sarlsattel 2229m

Our route took us south from the Edelweiss on a lane to the right from the main road. At a crossing of lanes to the east of Schmieden we continued south on the waymarked route 37 passing a small saw mill, with neat stacks of timber, before crossing the main road. We then continued on a track through pleasant woods to the west of the Stollabach. Some 2 km later route 37 leaves the lane for a nature trail

that passes crystal-clear spring-fed pools. After these pools the path rejoins the track, which leads to the main road. We turned northwards down the road and took the second opening to the right. This grassy track has a no entry sign for motors. After a while we approached a stream to our left. The Tabacco Map shows the track crossing the stream but it peters out without doing so. There was no problem crossing the stream and after a short walk through woods we reached a strada bianca that was footpath 14.

Some 0.3km further on 14 becomes a steep and narrow footpath heading south-eastwards climbing straight up the wooded hillside and shortcutting the looping strada bianca. Where the strada ends 14 becomes a broader well-made path that winds towards the east and then zigzags up to the Sarlriedle pass at 2099m. A weathered wooden fence runs along the ridge and to the east a cow pasture slopes down to woodland. The morning mists had given way to bright sunshine and we stopped to eat our sandwiches in the view of towering dolomite peaks to our right and left. Across the valley lay the massive outcrops where we were to walk the following day (opposite). From the col we followed footpath 33/Alta Via Dolomiti (AVD) 3. This heads north across the pasture and is easy walking until the steep but straightforward climb through scrub to our high point of the day – the Sarlsattle (below).

There are fine views from this col in all directions, but our way ahead seemed to involve a distinctly steep descent. In the event path 33 is well made and although it requires care as it winds down the rocky north face of the Sarlkofel it is not dangerous. Where eventually the path levels off and enters woods we headed right at a fork, still on 33/AVD 3 and soon reached the grassy Suisridl. There was a tight squeeze to get through the cattle-proof opening in a wooden fence here and then the path, still AVD 3, but now also footpath 16 descends NE through woods. This is an easy descent and the waymarked path joins and crosses a number of tracks. The complexity is accurately represented on the Tabacco map. After some time footpath 16 leaves the track to the left, but we continued on the track, now 16A. This eventually joins a metalled lane just above the hamlet of Saghäuser. Here we met a man on roller-skis descending at speed. Although we got out of his way in good time his guttural angry shouts as he sped past implied we had no right to be using the lane. With the exception of a group of mountain bikers on the way down to Lauterbrunen this was the only time on our traverse of the Alps when we were treated with anything but courtesy by others on the hills. On the far side of the houses at Saghäuser we turned right onto a strada bianca that heads south to the Toblacher See. At the north end of the lake there is a dramatic view (below) across the water to the narrow, deep and steep pass that leads south towards Cortina. We turned left across a bridge over the outlet from the lake to the Hotel Baur www.hotelbaur.it/en/. This delightful period building is set at the north-east corner of the lake. It was to provide our last bit of real luxury before Chimolais at the end of our sixth day of walking.

Day 73: Toblacher See to Drei Schusterhütte (1624m)
12.3km, up 1299m, down 939m, 5h30
High point the Birkenschartl 2531m

It is a relatively short distance to the Dreishusterhütte from the Toblacher See, but the climb to the Birkenschartl is long and there are some delicate sections on the descent from this col. The scenery throughout the day is spectacular. We walked down the path on the east side of the lake. The glassy surface was disturbed only by the occasional splash of a fisherman's lure. The path wound round the base of the lake and joined track 14, which led us south through well-kept woods. At a splitting of the track we turned left and passed a building with a humming electricity generator before reaching the main road. Here we turned left and after a short distance picked up the start of footpath 8 on the far side of the road. This path leads through woods to a broad dry river bed and then follows its north bank. We began to climb steeply following the clear red and white waymarks and after a while crossed branches of the river bed. Halfway up to the col the valley winds round from east to south east and the path goes through an unexpectedly large and pleasant patch of grassy woodland.

Eventually we came to the open scree of the upper valley, where a good path on the NE side of this cwm leads to the inevitable zigzags up the scree of the valley's headwall. High Dolomite cliffs that provided welcome shade soared magnificently on both sides of the cwm. We emerged into sunshine at the narrow gravely col known as the Birkenschartl and rested there taking in the fine views onwards to the sharp dolomite peaks of the Drei Zinnen range (above). We were going to walk among these the following day.

The descent from the col initially was steep and where there had been erosion to the path delicate. After the first 200m or so we reached a grassy patch where we relaxed and ate our sandwiches in the warm sun. After this pleasant break the waymarks led us across a steep gravelly bank high above the stream (below). This tricky detour seems to be unnecessary, for there is clearly an easier route on the other side of the stream. Eventually the path enters scrubby forest and descends the final section to the main valley floor on a well made path. The white dolomite stone of the broad and largely dry river bed below looks like unseasonal snow. Once in the valley it is a short walk north to the Drei Shusterhütte www.drei-schuster-huette.com/de/index.php.

Being a Saturday this large hut was busy and we were allocated births in a bunk-room set in the roof space. We obtained tokens for hot showers. JS and I enjoyed our showers, but there were loud protests when JD was left soaped-up with no water after he had inserted his token in the wrong meter slot.

While sorting out my things after the shower I realized that I had not collected my passport from the hotel we had stayed at the previous night. I asked the others if they had collected their documents and neither had. As there is no outgoing telephone from the hut we realized we would have to reach a point where we could contact the Hotel Baur and work out a means for being reunited with our passports. We were glad to learn that a shuttle bus runs from a point some 30 minutes' walk north down the valley. We packed up, paid for our showers and set off for the bus. This took us to the main road where we had mobile phone reception. I phoned the Hotel Baur and they already realized we had not been given our passports. They kindly offered to drive over with these. We were reunited with our documents half an hour later and had just enough time to catch the last bus back up the valley. After all the anxiety we were grateful to be back at the hut in time for welcome large beers and an excellent supper. It was rather hot in the bunk room during the night as the person with the berth nearest to the window insisted on keeping this closed. J S complained bitterly of a hazardous descent he needed to make down the loft ladder in the middle of the night.

Day 74: Dreischusterhütte to Rifugio Carducci (2312m)
14.0km, up 1353m, down 664m, 5h30
High point Büllelejoch 2561m

This classic high level walk traverses the Dolomiti de Sestro. Surprisingly the well made paths in the range made this one of our easiest and most secure walks. The weather was fair as we set off, retracing our steps up the west side of valley floor on the AVD 4 (105). Near the base of the valley's headwall we turned left across the scree of the dried river bed and then crossed a shallow feeder stream before starting up the wall. The well-made path climbs in zigzags through steep woodland. Half way up the wall the path crosses a stream and then climbs steeply again before reaching a small grassy hanging valley. This valley is surrounded by rocky walls and it is not clear at first where one can scale these. Nevertheless, wherever the path seemed likely to get difficult a hidden ledge appeared and progress up the rocks turned out to be totally straightforward. During this climb we had spectacular views back to the Birkenschartl, which we had crossed the day before (previous page). We reached a large plateau and crossed this to a col where the famous Drei Zinnen (Tre Chime) came into view across a wide deep cirque. These three massive spires were partially hidden in mist and the fine weather of the early morning was fading into gloom. There is a gentle descent from the col to the Drei Zinnenhütte (2405m) which is hidden round the back of a rocky peak – the Sextnerstein. As we approached the hut we met crowds of people who had come to watch a mountain running race. There was a loudspeaker blaring away. We hurried past the masses around the hut and set off on the path 101 that traverses above and to the south of the Bodenseen. The most southerly of these lakes is shown below. About half way along this path we started to meet runners coming in the opposite direction. Easily first

was an African athlete, who was clearly in a class of his own. We had to step off the path as each runner passed, which slowed our progress. The highest density of competitors came at the zigzag climb up to the

Büllelejochhütte. There I abandoned the path and scrambled up steep scree to avoid the racers. We stopped near the Büllelejochhütte to let the majority of runners pass before we tackled the safe rocky path that leads from the hut to the Oberbachernjoch. From this col there is a descent on a broad path round a pleasant cirque towards the Comichihütte. Just before the hut our route turns southeast on footpath 103 to the head of a deep gorge and then climbs diagonally on a good path up a massive scree slope to the Forcla Giralba (2431m) where we entered Italian speaking territory. The picture below shows JD approaching this Forcla.

It was misty at the col and raining lightly as we descended to the Rifugio Carducci www.rifugiocarducci.eu/. We were welcomed with

large beers which we sipped in front of a blazing fire. The guardian and his assistant both speak excellent English and seem to prefer not to speak German, emphasising that we had left the Südtyrol. We had hot showers and were allocated comfortable bunks. The evening meal was good, including excellent dumplings made with vegetables grown at 2312m. These were nettles picked from the alp around the hut. A well-fed wood burning stove in the day room was cheering and enabled us to dry our clothes.

Day 75: Rifugio Carducci to Refugio Ciareido (1969m)
17.7km, up 1099m, down 1431m, 6h23
High point at the Rifugio Carducci 2312m

It rained hard during the night and was still raining at breakfast. Consequently we put on our full rain gear, but when we stepped out of the rifugio, to our surprise and delight, the deluge had ceased. As we started our descent there was a hint of blue sky and miraculously within minutes we were in sunshine enjoying a wonderful morning. The

sunlight shimmered on the massive surrounding cliffs and the clouds were welling up from the valley (above). The 103/AVD 5 path from the hut to the mouth of the side valley is excellent and we made good progress on the long descent. In the main Val Giralba the scree and gravel at the base of the rocky cliffs that form the walls of the valley fall sharply to the river. Constant erosion has made it impossible to construct a track for farm vehicles, which may explain the remoteness of the upper valley and the absence of grazing animals. The way down to the road at Orsoligna is of continued interest. It crosses the unstable scree and at one point logs form a bridge over the torrent. A metal bridge with concrete supports upstream had been rendered useless by the river bank leading to it being washed away. As we continued down the valley the impressive peeks of the Marmarole Range towered ahead of us. We were heading into these hills later in the day (below).

On reaching the main road we turned left and came to a village where a cafe/restaurant served us panini with coffee on their terrace in the warm sunshine. A short way further down the road we turned right onto the metalled side-road, still AVD 5, which leads through forest up the Val da Rin. After 3km this lane passes the Primula Restaurant on the right. Surprisingly it was open on this Monday lunchtime in mid

September. Shortly after passing the restaurant the metalled road ends at a ford crossing the river. The water was sufficiently shallow for us to walk across without removing our boots. On the far side a track waymarked 273 led us to farm and forestry buildings at the Tabia da Rin. There path 273/AVD 5 goes to the right, but as this involves a delicate section above cliffs we chose to continue on the track. This climbs steadily up the north side of the Val de Poorse and provides a straightforward route to the high alp where the Rifugio Ciareido is located. At about 1600m the track levels off and there are great views back to the massive peaks of the Dolomiti de Sestro where we had walked the previous day. The track now divides and we took the right fork that traverses round the head of the valley and then climbs to near the base of the rocks of the Pian Deibuoy. Here we turned left onto the 28/237. A signpost at this point confusingly suggests the route to the Rifugio Ciareido is to the right, but it is in the opposite direction. We wondered if there is a conspiracy by the owners of the local cow pastures to avoid giving directions to the CAI Rifugio Ciareido, for the rival private Baion hut is linked to a cattle farm. Happily the Tabacco map proved reliable. After a while 28/237 joins the 268 and shortly after this a lane labelled 28 on the map leaves to the right (west) and climbs to the Ciareido. There was no reference to the Rifugio Ciareido at either of these turnings, but a prominent sign advertised the Rifugio

Baion at a turning to the left off the 28. Further on where the 28 enters woodland there is at last a notice about the Rifugio Ciareido. From there it is a stiff climb up the lane, which is metalled in places, to the rocky outcrop where the Rifugio Ciareido is located www.rifugiociareido.com. For some reason the Johns raced up this last section to the hut. I proceeded more slowly enjoying the late afternoon sunshine. On arriving a large, very welcome beer was waiting for me. I drank this in front to the rifugio, while admiring the view of the magnificent Spalti de Toro hills to the south (above), our destination the following day. We were the only people staying at the Rifugio and after a hot shower, enjoyed a good meal and comfortable night.

Day 76: Rifugio Ciareido to Rifugio Padova (1287m)
18.6km, up 1261m, down 1932m, 6h55
High point below il Pupo 1993m

It was a misty atmospheric morning when we set off. The hills that we were going to approach later in the day emerged from time to time through breaks in the cloud. Between us and these hills lay a seemingly very deep valley which reflects the long descent we were facing.

We headed west from the rifugio joining the AVD 5/273 and following this to the left. Initially this is a broad well-made path that climbs gently under the rocky peaks of Monte Ciastelin, but after a while the 273 forks left. We followed this muddy narrow path as it meanders up and down across cow pasture and scrubby woodland. On reaching a forested ridge the path heads downhill steeply. The mud in this section was pretty treacherous and it was a relief when we reached the less steep cow pasture surrounding the Rifugio Baion with its large cowsheds. We passed these buildings and then followed path 264, descending across an east-facing wooded hillside, soon reaching a narrow track (above). This took us down to the Forcla Bassa, some 250m below the Rifugio Baion. The track then climbs gently to the base of a hill, where 264 leaves as a path to the right that zigzags steeply upwards. At around 1700m the path joins a track and passes a couple of wooden buildings. We were now on the start of the Cresta de Croda. After a while the track again becomes a path and descends to a narrow grassy plateau with a white rock face to the right and steep hillside on the left. There were a number of small wooden summer houses to the left of the path that have a fine view south-eastwards across the valley. Beyond the houses the plateau narrows to a ridge and the almost horizontal path follows its crest. Eventually the ridge broadens once again and the path joins a track that winds down through forest losing a long 700m before reaching Grea. We passed several shuttered summer houses located in clearings in the forest along this track.

Grea is a pleasant village on the hillside above the Lago di Centro Cadore. After the first hairpin bend on the main road from Grea to the valley floor we took a lane to the left. This led to the busy main road in Vallesella. We crossed this road and headed down towards a narrow concrete bridge over the lake. It had been a tiring descent and we were glad to find a cafe across a park to the right before the bridge. This served us satisfying toasted sandwiches. After the welcome lunch we crossed the bridge and followed a track, labelled VA, to the left through the woods. The track wound round the hillside climbing a little before traversing to the river flowing through Val Talagona. We were frustrated to see that the stone bridge across the river has been washed away, but our despair was short-lived as we were able to cross the torrent on a temporary wooden footbridge. On the far side a path climbs through woods leading to the metalled lane that winds up the east side of the valley. This took us through beautiful woodland to the Rifugio Padova (above). It is charming family-run rifugio in a period building www.rifugiopadova.it. The surrounding lawns are decorated with wood carvings of exceptional quality. The family made us very welcome and allocated us to a 4-berth bunk room, which we had to ourselves. The only other people staying at the rifugio that night were two elderly (well about our age) German-speaking gentlemen, one of whom was playing chess with the guardian's youngest son.

Day 77: Rif. Padova to Cimolais, Albergo Margherita (650m)
21.6km, up 1243m, down 1885m, 6h30
High point Forcla Montfalcon 2309m

After overnight rain there was clear blue sky as we headed east up the drive from the rifugio. Where this loops round the valley to the left we continued straight ahead on path 346 climbing to the east through beech woods. The path took us round the hillside into the Val d'Arade. There is a steep climb up this valley on dolomite scree through scrub battered by a previous avalanche. Many saplings had had their trunks snapped by the rushing snow. After this steep section we entered a hanging valley and crossed scree to a further island of scrubby ground. Beyond this the path leads to the scree of the left side of the cirque and from there to the base of a cliff in the valley headwall. We passed in front of the cliff and then climbed steeply in zigzags up scree to the Forcla Montfalcon. Beyond is a magical high cirque with two further cols in its rim. We were to visit both. The weather was perfect and we were able to savour one of the most remote and beautiful areas of high mountain scenery visited on the whole of our alpine traverse. From the col we walked east across a grassy slope to the Forcla da las Basas (above). Then we turned to the south and traversed downwards across the steep scree under the Cima Barbe (background of the photo below) until we arrived at the grassy base of the cirque. There we again turned and this time climbed to the west up steep scree to the Forcla del Leone (page 151 and below). On the far side of this col, path 394 traverses high across the scree of the east flank of the valley before descending to grassy meadow. The relaxed walking on grass was not to last, for the lower half of the valley is a long slope of ankle-testing scree. Some 100m above the end of the valley the 394 leaves the scree to the south-west and then traverses across steep beech forest to the Rifugio Pordone. Here we stopped for some lunch before setting off on the 13km walk to the village of Cimolais.

Although this stage of the walk is on a road it passes through a beautiful and impressive valley that is part of the Parco delle Dolomiti Friulane. There was almost no traffic and we were gently aided by gravity. The hills on either side of the valley rise precipitously, while the valley floor consists of mixtures of pasture and woodland that lie on either side of a broad dry stony river bed. The road swings to and fro across the valley crossing the river bed a number of times. Where the valley passes through a rocky gorge the river emerges above ground. In this section the road crosses three bridges over the torrent. After the gorge the valley heads south and we passed the park entrance. Soon the road climbs to the right, but we continued by the river on a broad stony track for the last 3km into Cimolais. Once in this village we continued to the main road where on the far side to the left we found our hotel – the Albergo Ristorante Margherita di Protti +39 0427 87060. We were given two comfortable adjacent rooms one twin and the other single. The restaurant does not seem to have a web site, but the owner speaks excellent English so a booking is easily made by 'phone.

Day 78: Cimolais to Rifugio Casera Ditta (956m)
12.7km, up 798m, down 479m, 4h05
High point the Pian di Mesazzo 991m

After two long walks we were glad to have a relatively short day and took advantage of this by breakfasting at 8 am, an hour later than normal. Our route headed west from the hotel climbing on the main road through pleasant woods to the Passo di S Osvaldo (820m). Here a huge rusted iron cross stands by the south side of the road. As we started to descend on the far side of the pass we could see ahead the bare rock slabs of the fateful Monte Toc. In 1963 the large part of this mountain that overlaid the slabs fell into the barraged Lago del Vajont. This caused a massive destructive tidal wave that swept over the dam at the end of the lake destroying the villages in the valley below. The death toll was estimated at over 2000. Although the 262m high dam remains intact the east end of the lake is filled in by the landslide and the water level is kept some 150m below the top of the dam. The dam has never again been used to generate electricity. A little over a km after the pass we took a lane to the left that loops round the previous east end of the lake. After the lane turns to the west it crosses an impressive bridge over a deep gorge and then goes through a tunnel. Some 4 km further on the lane loops to the left twice as it crosses two torrents that flow into the lake from the south. After the crossing the second torrent the lane goes through another tunnel and then loops to the north as it passes through Pineda. On the far side of this hamlet we turned left (south) onto the clearly sign-posted footpath 905/AVD 6. This path climbs through beech woods on the west side of the Val Mezas. After reaching 900m the path joins a pleasant contouring forest track, which we followed for about 1.5km until its end. The Tabacco map is inaccurate here, for it shows the track ending after less than half a km. At the end of the track we came across the parked blue Fiat Panda of the guardian of the Rifugio Casera Ditta. He told us later that he carries all the supplies to the hut from this parking place on his back. The path to the rifugio descends to and crosses a stream. It then works its way down to Mezas River and crosses this by a rickety wooden bridge before climbing to the Rifugio Casera Ditta (below). This rifugio www.rifugiocaseraditta.com/main.htm is surrounded by fine lawns cropped by pet rabbits of the guardian. He speaks excellent English and served us a lunch of cold meats and cheese, which we ate on the terrace. There were no other visitors to the refugio that day. Washing facilities are a cold tap in the garden and the outside toilets require squatting, but in other respects our stay was comfortable and we were fed well. The rifugio has its own hydroelectric generator, which provides ample electric light and keeps the living room warm. The guardian is clearly a passionate rock climber. He warned us that the route 905 over the Forcla del Lastra was tricky. When we went to bed he was waiting with a rifle in his kitchen hoping to take a shot at the fox that had been killing his lawnmowers.

Day 79: Rifugio Casera Ditta to Refugio Dolada (1488m)
7.9km, up1316m, down 777m, 7h00
High point Col Mat 1981m

Despite the warnings we set off on the 905, for probably the most challenging day of our traverse of the Alps. The path heads south from the rifugio and crosses the dry bed of a side stream before turning left up the east bank of the Mezas Stream. The red and white waymarked path crosses this stream a number of times. It then climbs up its right flank successively passing through a beech wood and across grassy banks and a number of side steams before turning into a steep boulder-filled gully that leads to the Forcla della Meda. There is a small patch of mixed woodland on the north side of this col, but on the south side the way forward is a traverse on a barely detectable path on steep ground above precipitous cliffs. Waymarks were the main indicator of the route as in places the path was absent. We crept across this delicate traverse for some two or three hundred meters before turning a spur and making an exposed descent into a gully, where we at last felt reasonably safe. The next section continues the traverse, but now on more rocky ground (above). Although some of the rock was fragmented we felt a little more secure here. Eventually we started to climb to the left up a gully and reached a moderately-angled rocky face. Where the angle of

the ascent increased we came across the first of 4 sections of via ferrata. This at last enabled completely secure progress. After two via ferrata sections there was more free scrambling up a steep gully (below) and its right-hand wall. There were two more sections of via ferrata before more scrambling up to the grassy Forcla della Lastra. From here we could at last see the Adriatic. There was little evidence of traffic over this col and the guardian at the Rifugio Dolata estimated perhaps no more than 10 parties would use this route in a season.

From the forcla we made our way down steep grass to the "path" that traverses below the ridge. We headed south on this indistinct path climbing on steep tufted grass and sections of rock to the Forcla Galina. The map indicates an easier traverse from here to the right of the crest of the Col Mat (col in this context refers to a summit rather than a pass). A notice was placed a short way along this route to say it was no longer passable. Consequently we took the allegedly more difficult route over the sharp crest of the Col Mat (opposite). There was minimal wind and the conditions were dry. Consequently the traverse of the ridge proved much less problematical than our route of the morning. At the low point between the Col Mat and the Col Dolomieu we took a path to the left that traverses across the steep grassy slope below the crest of the ridge. This path leads back to the 905 where it goes between the Forcla Dolada and the rifugio where we were going to stay. The traversing path presented no serious difficulty and on reaching path 905 we continued the short walk through conifer woods to the Rifugio Dolomieu al Dolada www.rifugiodolada.it.

We were expected by the guardian, who speaks excellent English. Reassuringly he had already been called by his colleague from the Casera Dita enquiring whether we had arrived, and he phoned back to confirm that we had. The Rifugio Doloda is a fine building with magnificent views across the valley to the east. After being refreshed with a beer and some apple strudel we were allocated a comfortable bedroom. We had hot showers and then went down to the large sitting room on the first floor, which also had a roaring fire. Picture windows in this room gave wonderful views of the Col Nuda and the Monte Cavallo ranges. The Santa Croce lake was also visible with the hill rising from its north-eastern shore that we were to traverse on our final approach to Vittorio Veneto. We were fed well and had a comfortable night. This rifugio is certainly worth a return visit.

Day 80: Refugio Dolada to Rifugio Semenza (2020m)
21.9km, up 1588m, down 1061m, 7h23
High point the Forcla Laste 2044m

From the rifugio we set off on path 509. This descends through the woods in long zigzags leading to the Staol di Plois. We headed north-east from the hamlet on a metalled road. After about half a km the road forks and we took the lane to the right, which soon becomes a strada bianca. This pleasant track continues north-eastwards parallel to, but some 1000m below the ridge we had traversed the previous day. After passing a stream where there had been some road improvements we came to another fork. The left branch is the end of the AVD 6 that comes down from the Forcla di Lastra, which we had crossed the previous day. We took the right track, which leads round the head of the valley, becomes a lane and then descends SE towards the Village of San Martino. From there the walk continues through the pleasant villages of Funes and Irrighe. After the last of these villages we started to climb again to the village of Mont. At this stage there were fine views back to the Col Mat ridge and across the valley to the Santa Croce lake and the final hills before the Adriatic (above).

We followed the road to the closed Agrotourismo Cate and from there headed up footpath 924. This shortcuts the metalled lane that leads up to the Val Salatis. The 924 joins the road as it levels off and becomes a track. On reaching the Cabin ra Pian de la Stale we left the track and climbed up a grassy slope south-eastwards to the entry to an ancient stream course. The rocky walls and floor of the pathway show signs of smoothing by water erosion. The path opens out into a heath-land valley and passes some deep sink holes before reaching a scree slope that leads to the narrow entrance to the upper Val Salatis. The path continues across the scree on the right side of the upper valley before climbing a grassy headwall with rocky outcrops and reaching the

Forcla Laste. From there we had magnificent views north over the hills we had crossed during the previous week (above). It is two minutes to the south from the col to the Rifugio Semenza, www.rifugiosemenza.it/rifugio.html (next page). We were welcomed once again with apple strudel and beer. The hut was full at supper time, but all bar 5 of us left after the meal for a descent to the road-head in the dark.

Day 81: Rifugio Semenza to Pian del Cansiglio (1013m)
16.2km, up 298m, down 1289m 5h20
High point the Rifugio Semenza 2020m

It was a misty start, but we soon got below the clouds and then came sunshine. The start of the walk from the rifugio traverses on the right side of the valley between the top of a scree slope and the base of a cliff. After half a km we took a left fork, still on 923 that descends on steep scree to the foot of the hanging valley. There the box cable car supplying the hut has an intermediate pylon. The path then traverses round the end of the left side of the valley into the next valley where it

descends to the Cabina ra Palantina, which is set in pasture. Here we picked up the 922 path, heading south-west into forest and following the crest of a broad ridge between the Val de Piera and the Val Bella. The beauty of the beech forest on either side of this path made the walk down to the roadhead at Canaie enchanting. We turned left at the buildings at Canaie and followed the road south through a couple of right turns and then a left bend before leaving the road at the next right turn for a track heading southwards. This track is labelled the Sentaro Alpago Natura on the map and is barred to motors. It winds through forest, eventually descending eastwards before coming to a three-way junction. Here we turned right and descended westwards on a potholed metalled lane, labelled route B. After just over a km we turned left onto a track that heads east and then almost immediately right onto a grassy path labelled route A. This climbs south-westwards through woods.

After ascending about 100m the path falls to and crosses a track before climbing again to a similar height and then joining a road, marked on the map as A-B. We turned right onto this road and headed west out of the wood onto the Pian de Cansiglio. After crossing a golf course we reached the main road. On the far side of this road to the left we reached the Albergo/Rifugio San Osvaldo in time for an excellent Sunday lunch including delicious wild fungi. We enjoyed our stay at this comfortable Albergo www.albergosantosvaldo.it/eng.

Day 82: Pian del Cansiglio to Vittorio Veneto (138m)
19.5km, 818m up, 1693m down, 6h30
High point Monte Pizzoc 1565m

On the final day we set off on a lane that runs west from the south side of the Albergo. This climbs gently to a grassy path that continues into the woods on the west flank of the Pian de Cansiglio. Here we headed south on footpath S through beech wood to a cluster of buildings at Vallorch. From there we took footpath F1 climbing through more beech woods. By now the sun had broken through the mist and the straight white trunks of the tall beeches were elegantly dappled with sunbeams (above). Eventually F1 enters a steep muddy gorge, which we climbed to the traversing path H, which leads to the summit of the ridge. This path winds round a spur and then traverses high on the flank of a wooded valley. We came out of the woods just below the ridge and climbed past two houses to the crest. There are fine views from the ridge down to the Lago Santa Croce 1250m below and across to the hills where we had been walking between the refugios Casera Dita, Dolada and Semenza. After a detour to the somewhat barren summit of Monte Pizzoc we retraced our steps to the start of the path marked 980 on the map, but signed as TV1 on the ground. This well-made path winds down a ridge towards Vittorio Veneto. Waymarking is erratic and the meaning of those waymarks that are present is unclear. Nevertheless, the path coincides closely with the way it is depicted on the Tabacco map. At about 1100m the path winds round from the south-west to the south-east and descends through coppiced woods on the side of the ridge. At the Col Bressan the path levels off and then traverses round the left flank of a wooded hill. After descending to a track we turned right and headed more or less horizontally west and then south-west. About a km further on, after the track winds round to the left, we followed a path that leads off to the right. This path descends with occasional short climbs to the church of Santa Augusta. The last section before the church is quite steep and the drop from a step or two to the left of the path is precipitous.

We rested at the church for a while in the warm afternoon sun thankful that we had completed our long walk from Menton without misadventure. It then only remained for us to descend the last 200m on the stone staircase (above) followed by a zigzagging stone-paved lane that lead down to the old town of Vittorio Veneto.

The descent ends with a final grand double staircase at the top of which stands a statue of Santa Augusta, an innocent maid who was martyred for her Christian faith in 409AD by her father. When we reached the bottom of the stairs it was time to take a group photograph (below) before proceeding to the Hotel Terme www.hotelterme.tv in the newer part of town near the railway station.

It had taken us 82 life-changing days to complete our grand traverse of the Alps. The scenery, of course was magnificent, but we had found wonderful remoteness as well as great companionship. The weather was nearly always kind and we had stayed in a great variety of places where we had met interesting and friendly people. Although we were six years older by the time we came to visit Santa Augusta in many ways we felt more youthful.

After the walk

The following morning we took the train for the short journey to Venice Santa Lucia. It did not seem appropriate to trudge across the Venetian plane a few feet above sea level to end our long walk across the Alps. In Venice we met up with our wives, who had rented an apartment on the lagoon overlooking the glass-making Island of

Murano. Beyond were views back to the hills that had engaged our attention over the previous several days. It was a pleasant way to finish our long walk through the Alps from Menton. Finally two days later we closed up the flat and took the Alilaguna Blue Line Launch from the Fondamente Nove to the airport and from there flew home.

JS resting and Ian writing outside the Etzlihütte at the end of Day 46

APPENDIX

When to walk

The season for this walk is dictated by the dates most of the alpine huts are open. In general this is between mid June and mid September. Although the second half of June and early July is a great time to be in the hills snow may be a problem. Even so an ice axe and light instep crampons may provide sufficient protection for the route described in this book. The first two weeks in September has proved a good time to walk. The hills are less busy than in July and August and the walking conditions are often good in terms of temperature and absence of steep snow. Mid July to mid August provide good conditions, but huts can be crowded and booking essential.

Mapping

The French IGN maps are available electronically from Ordinance Survey Memory Map www.memory-map.co.uk/. These can of course also be obtained through IGN, but be warned that the memory map and IGN software are not compatible, so all your maps should be purchased through one or the other. The IGN maps I have bought of the Ardech and Cevennes require the user to have a DVD in the computer. The software may be less restrictive now.

Two Memory Map IGN 1:25k discs are required for the Menton to Lake Geneva stretch of the walk: "Provence, Côte d'Azure, Mediterranée et Corse" covers Menton to the South end of the Queyras Alps, while "les Alpes" covers the northern stretch to Lake Geneva.

The programme allows you to draw your routes and work out the distance, height gain and height loss. After drawing the route I print this out at 1:25k double-sided on A4 paper. This saves a lot of weight compared with using the commercially-printed IGN maps.

Swiss maps are available free online through the "Swiss Mobility" web site. http://map.wanderland.ch/. It is worth purchasing the draw facility on this site. It will allow you to work out your route and store this online. It costs about 30 Swiss francs a year for this facility. You can also download A4-sized Swiss maps of your choice as PDF files. If you have PDF write software you can crop and annotate the maps. These maps will also suffice for the sections in north-eastern Lombardy between Pontresina and the Stilfser Joch (Days 57-59).

When we did the walk there were no electronic versions of the 1:25k Tabacco maps of north eastern Italy. I purchased printed maps, scanned A4-sized sections from these and made annotated PDF files for our walks across the Südtyrol and Veneto Dolomites. Amazon sell these maps at an appreciably lower price than specialist map shops. Eleven maps cover Days 59-82: Map 8 (Days 59-61), Map 45 (Days 61 & 62), Map 42 (Days 63 & 64), Map 46 (Days 64 & 65), Map 40 (Days 65 & 66), Map 5 (Days 67-68), Map 7 (Days 68-70) Map 31 (Days 68-72), Map 10 (Day 72-75), Map 17 (Days 74 & 75), Map 16 (Days 76, 77), Map 21 (Days 77 & 78), Map 12 (Days 79-82). For a list of these maps see http://www.tabaccoeditrice.it/eng/map_area.asp?cat=1. Recently digital versions of these maps have become available for PC & MAC at http://www.tabaccomapp.it/en/.

The "Walking and Hiking in the Südtyrol" web site www.trekking.suedtirol.info/ has been invaluable for planning walks in this Italian province. It shows all the footpaths in the Südtyrol and it is easy to work out routes. It is free to register so that you can store the routes you want to walk. The detail on these maps is not good enough to use for walking so they have to be used in conjunction with the Tabacco Map scans.

Most of the GR paths in the French Alps are now shown, although not labelled, on Google Earth. Google Earth has a route drawing facility. When I have cross-checked this against Memory Map calculations the results of the two systems are remarkably comparable. This gave me confidence to use Google Earth-drawn routes in the Veneto Dolomites to calculate distances and height gains and losses.

Points of entry and exit from the walk

These hints about where the walk can be entered or left are listed in series from Menton to Vittorio-Veneto

Menton is served by good rail links from on both the French and Italian side. The nearest airport is at Nice.

Day 1,2: Sospel has a branch-line rail link to and from Nice

Day 4,5: From la Madone de Fenestre one can walk to St Martin Vesubie from where there is a good inexpensive bus service to the Airport and Railway Station at Nice

Day 5,6: From le Boréon one can walk or bus to St Martin Vesubie and take the bus to Nice Airport or Railway Station

Day 16, 17: Briançon has good rail links to Aix en Provence, Lyon and Marseille

Day 18: Modane has excellent rail links to both the French and Italian rail networks

Day 22, 23: The Auberge Valezan lies 6km west of the railway station at Aime la Plagne. This is along the D86 and involves a 600m ascent.

Day 24: The Mt Blanc Tramway provides a link to the main rail network at St Gervais les Bains

Day 29,30: There are links from St Gingolph by boat to Lausanne and Vevey, where there are main line stations. There is also a rail branch line to St Gingolph that links to the main line along the Rhône Valley at Aigle.

Day 31,32: The mainline railways station at Aigle is a short distance south of Yvorne

Day 32,33: The branch line to les Diablerets links to the main line at Aigle

Day 38: There is a main-line station at Kandersteg

Day 40,41,42: The branch-line stations at Lauterbrunnen and Grindelwald link with the main line at Interlaken

Day 42,43: The rail links from Meiringen go to main-line stations at both Lucerne and Interlaken

Day 45,46: Erstfeld has a main-line station

Day 47: There is a branch-line station at Sedrun that links to the main-line stations at Chur and Göshenen

Day 52: The walk passes near the main-line station at Thusis

Day 55,56: The station at St Moritz is about 5km NE of Surlej and links to the mainline at Thusis

Day 56,57: The station at Pontresina links to the main line at Thusis

Day 65: The railway line from the station at Lana Postal links to the main line to Verona, Innsbruck and Munich at Bozen/Bolzano

Day 67: Klausen/Chiusa is on the main line between Verona, Innsbruck and Munich

Day 71,72: The branch line from the station at Niederdorf/Villabassa links at Frazensfeste/Fortezza to the main line between Verona, Innsbruck and Munich.

Day 82: There are connections from Vittorio Vento station to Venice.

Finding and Booking accommodation

The accommodation we used on this walk is set out at the end of each day's account. In most cases the web site of the lodging is given, but where this is not available a telephone number or email address is provided. These web sites were all operational in April 2014. We have always booked accommodation in advance. This is particularly important at weekends when huts may be full. Even if the hut is not full booking gives the warden time to make sure food is in stock and may set alarm bells ringing if a party fails to arrive.

Sometimes it is necessary to pay a deposit, which is easy if a debit card number is accepted. This is the case for many of the CAF huts and most, but not all hotels. Sometimes other lodgings ask for a cheque. I have always managed to persuade such lodgings that this is impracticable from the UK and offer to pay by bank transfer. Often they wave the deposit at this stage, but if they want a transfer this can be done from a British Bank to a European Bank for a fee of about £10. Although this is expensive for one person it is not too bad if you are a group of four walkers. The name and address of the account holder as well as those of the bank are required together with both the BIC and IBAN numbers of the recipient's account.

Hopefully this guide will take the hard work out of finding accommodation, but if you want to find alternatives the first thing to do is to find a location where you want to obtain lodging using maps, and Google Earth. Then look for lodgings using the web. Ideally try and obtain the web site of the lodging itself. I try to avoid a booking agency unless it is used by the lodging place itself e.g. Logis de France.

Wherever possible try and get confirmation from the lodging by email and take a copy of this with you. It is then impossible for the lodging to say you have no booking. I speak reasonable French, but in German and Italian speaking regions I have found Google Translate https://translate.google.co.uk/ works pretty well and often the lodging will reply in English anyway.

Most huts and many gîtes d'étapes will only accept payment in cash, so ensure you have sufficient Euros.

Equipment

Every walker will have their own equipment preferences, but it may be helpful to list the kit I take on a two week walk in the Alps.

1 rucksack 45-50L. This should give plenty of room for your kit. I use a 48 litre Osprey Kestrel.
1 waterproof rucksack liner
1 waterproof rucksack cover
I pair Gortex-lined mid-height light-weight walking boots
I pair of shoes for evenings I use GTX light-weight trainers, which can act as a back-up for boots if the former get waterlogged. Many of the walks described can be done in trainers.
3 pairs of cotton rich of socks that will dry overnight after washing
2 light-weight quick-dry short-sleeved walking shirts
1 light-weight quick-dry long-sleeved shirt for evenings
1 pair shorts; these are the usual attire for walking and in poor weather are a better base to the Gortex shell outer trousers than long trousers
1 pair long walking trousers for travelling and evenings
3 pairs quick-dry boxer shorts
1 light-weight microfleece jumper
1 light-weight Gortex shell top
1 pair light-weight Gortex shell trousers
1 thermal vest to sleep in and as an extra layer in emergencies
1 sun hat
1 pair photosensitive glasses or sun glasses
1 pair fleece gloves
1 fleece balaclava. You may never use this but it could be helpful in an emergency
1 light-weight quick-dry camping towel
1 light-weight cloth to cover hut pillows
1 silk sheet sleeping bag
1, 1 litre water bottle

1 led light head torch with new batteries
1 sponge bag with 50ml toothpaste, tooth brush, bar soap (for washing clothes and yourself), nail brush (doubles as hair brush), plasters, nail scissors, ear plugs (bunk rooms can be noisy), a thin 3m clothes line, needle and thread, light weight pen knife.
High factor sun cream
Compass
Watch preferably with an altimeter
Pocket camera e.g Cannon Powershot S120, 2 2Gb memory cards. With 2 spare batteries you will not need to carry a charger.
Kindle; fully charged this should last a fortnight's walk
Mobile phone + charger and adaptor
Maps
Boarding passes
Record of Bookings
Train tickets
Wallet, Currency, health insurance card, Visa debit card, Mastercard
Passport
Route schedule
4 Small self-sealing polythene bags
1 A4 self-sealing map folder to store all the maps and papers
1 A5 self-sealing map folder for the day's maps
A small notebook and ball-point pen to keep a log
In late June consider taking an ice axe and instep crampons.
Many people find a pair of walking poles useful. I used these in the last four stages of our walk.
The above equipment should give you a packed rucksack which weighs comfortably under 9kg.

INDEX

Aiguille(s):
  de Bacque 49
  de Chambeyron 6, 30
  du Grand Fond 54
  les Miettes 71
  de Tortisse 26
Aigle, town 74, 181
Aime la Plagne, SNCF 52, 181
Albergo: see Auberge, Albergo
Alp
  Carschenna 112, 113
  Crocs 113
  Digl Plaz 116
  Flix 116
  Natons 116
  da Stretta 122, 123
Alpine Passes trail 107
Alps Maritime 6-29
Alta Via Dolomiti (AVD):
  AVD 3, 153
  AVD 4, 157
  AVD 5, 160-165
  AVD 6, 167, 172
Ammertegrat (ridge) 81
Ammerte Shafberg 81
Amsteg, village 100
Antoniusjoch 146
Archas, Mount 18
l'Are, Chalet de 56
l'Arpette, Pas de 14
l'Arpille, Arête de 77

Artelgrat 83
Auberge, Albergo:
  de Couranne, Yvorne 74
  du Barrage du Sanetsch 77
  Margherita di Protti 167
  de l'Ours, Vers l'Eglise 75
  de la Poste, les Diablerets 75
  Provençal, Sospal 9
  Valezan 50, 52
Auener Alm 138
Auener Jöchl 138
Ausser Pilsberg Alm 132
Ausserraschotz, plateau 142
Aussersulden, village 129
Aussois, town 38, 43-45
l'Authion 6, 9, 11-12
Ayères des Pierrières 58
Ayères des Rocs 58

Badia, town 145
Baisse:
  de Camp d'Argent 6, 9, 11
  de Caveline 13
  de Cinq Lacs 15
  de la Déa 11
  definition of 9
  de Liniere 11
  de Prais 15
  de St Véran 13
la Balme, restaurant 55
Balmegghorn 94, 95
Baraquements de Viraysse 29

Beaufort Alps 50-54
Beaupraz, hamlet 51
Bec de Roux 30
Bellentre, village 51
Belvedere de la Mourière 33
Beischen Plaz, Hamlet 115
Berggasthaus Pederü 120, 146-148
Berghaus Bärtschi 82
Berghaus Beverin 111
Berghaus Iffigenalp 69, 79, 80
Bernese Oberland 86-96
Bernina mountain railway 122
Bionnassay, Glacier 56
Birkenscarte 154, 155, 158
Bivio, Village 92, 115-117
Blockitobel canyon 99
Blüemlisalp 67, 68, 84-86
BMRES 1
Bodenseen 158
Bog Orchids 116
Bouquetin 46
Brec de Chambeyron 30
Briançon 1-3, 5, 6, 35-41, 181
Bristantobel gorge 100
Brochaux, les 61
Brocchetta di Forcola 126
Brunissard, village 35
Buffère, Chalets de 40
Brüsti cable car station 99
Bütlasse 86

Cabane des Audannes 77, 79
Camona see: Hut, Hütte
Campi, hamlet 112
Canaie, hamlet 174
Canale Torto 124
Capulota farm 117
Cascade de Combe Noire 55
Cavoria, village 103

Ceillac 6, 32-34
Chablais Alps 60-73
Chalet(s):
　des Ayes 35
　de Buffère 40
　de Miage 55
　-Refuge de Rosuel 50
　du Truc 55
　de Vers le Col 36
la Chalp-Arvieux 6, 34, 35
Chapelle d'Abondance 38, 62-63
la Chapelle des Ammes 41
Chapelle St-Pierre 47
Charmaix, Village 44
Châtelard, Tunnel du 58
Château Queyras 34
Chaux Palin 61
Chavanette ski wall 61
Chemin Claudius Bernard 55
Chemin de l'Energie 24
Cheval Blanc (peak) 43
Cime, Cima:
　Barbe 166
　du Diable 12
　de la Gonella 11
　du Mangiabo 11
　de Piagu 16, 17
　du Pisset 17
　de Raus 13
　du Ters 10
　de Tuis 11
Cimolais village 150, 165-167
Cholplatz 100
Clarive, Hameau de 70
Col:
　d'Antern 58, 59
　des Audannes 77, 78
　des Ayes 35
　du Barbier 44
　de Bassechaux 62

Col continued:
  Barteaux 40
  du Berceau 8
  de Bise 64, 71
  du Bonhomme 55
  du Bresson 53
  Bressan 176
  de Chésery 61
  de Coux 61
  de la Croix 71
  de la Croix du Bonhomme 55
  Dolomieu 170
  des Eaux Froides 79
  de Fer 26
  de Forclaz 58
  Fromage 34
  de la Golèse 60
  de Granon 40
  de la Guercha 22
  d'Izoard 35
  du Lausfer 21
  de la Leisse 48
  de la Lombarde 20
  de Mallemort 29
  Mat 168, 170, 172
  de Mercière 19
  du Palet 48
  de Pauriac 27
  du Pillon 75
  de Raus 13
  du Rawil 82
  de Razet 8
  de Saboule 21
  de Salèse 17
  de Sanetsch (Senein) 77
  de la Sauce 54
  la Selle 79
  de Serenne 30, 31
  de Thorse 42
  de Tricot 55
  la Turra 45

  du Vallonnet 29
  de la Vanoise 47
  de Voza 56
Colla Bassa 7, 8
Colle Longue, Pas de 23
Collet de Tortisse 26
Colombe, Agence de 20
Combe d'Armancette 55
les Contamines Montjoie 55
Cormet de Roselend 54
Cornettes de Bise 63, 64, 71
Coston Sulden, Village 128, 130
la Couletta, Pas de 29, 30
Crap Alo 104
Cresta de Croda 163
Crête:
  d'Andreveysson 33
  des Babarottes 24, 25
  de Coincon 62
  des Gittes 55
  Malefosse 37
  de la Mourière 33
  de la Selle 34
Croix de la Chime 40
Croix des Dammes 70
Croix de Toulouse 37
Crocs, Alp 113
Cumbel, Town 109
Curaglia 104

Dents du Midi, les 61, 73
Dent Parrachée 44, 45
les Diablerets 67, 69, 74, 75
Digl Plaz Alp 116
Dolomites 121, 143-174
Dolomiti de Sestro 157-161
Dôme de l'Arpont 47
Drei-Sprachen-Spitz 125-126
Drei Zinnen (Tre Chime) 155, 158 166

Durance valley, view of 39
Duvin 109

Écrins 1, 31, 32, 39
Eggeschwand 83
Eiger 69, 86, 89, 90
Engadine see Val Engiadin
Engleberg, town 97
Engstlenalp 92, 94-96
Engstlensee 97
Engstligenalp 69, 80, 82
Erstfeld, town 92, 98-100
Escreins, Vallon, Pic d' 32

Faix, Hameau les 60
Figist 142
Fiz, Rochers de 59
Flix, Alp 116
Fond des Joux, dairy 76
Fonteklaus 142
Forcla:
  da las Basas 165
  Bassa 163
  Dolada 171
  Galina 170
  Giralba 159
  della Lastra 170
  Laste 172,173
  del Leone 151, 166
  della Meda 169
  Montfalcon 165
  Surlej 93, 118
la Forclaz, Village 74, 75
Forclaz, Col de 58
Frazensfeste/Fortezza 182
Fort des Sallettes 37
Fouillouse, village 6, 29, 30
Fragrant Orchids 95
Frejus, tunnels 44
Frentschenberg, hamlet 100

le Freney, Hameau 70
Friulane, Parco 166
Funes, village 172
Fuorcla da Lavaz 104
Fuorcla Sura da Lavaz 104-107

Gamchigletscher 85, 86
Garvan 5, 7
Gnoll, Gasthoff 142
Geisler Odel 144
Guesthouse see: Hotel, Pension,
Giagiabella, Mont 9
Gîte d'Étape:
  les Baladins 33
  du Boréon 17
  le Chalet Viso 35
  le Châtelet 58
  le Corborant 24
  le Creux des Souches 41
  l'Estive du Mercantour 11
  Grand Traverse des Alps 28
  les Granges, Fouillouse 30
Glatscher da Lavaz, 106
Goldring, banhoff, 133
Graf Walkmar Weg, 137
Gande Randonée
  GR5, 2, 24, 27-65
  GR5c, 37-40
  GR52, 2, 7-18
  GR55, 47-49
  GR57, 41
  GR58, 32, 33
Grand, village, 132
Grande Casse, 47
Grande Motte, la, 38, 46, 47, 49
la Grande Peyrolle 37, 40
Grat, ridge 99
Grea, village 164
Grindelwald 69, 88, 89, 181

Grosse Scheidegg 89, 94
Grund 89
Grüner Baum Inn 138
Grünwaldalm 149
Gsteig, village 75, 76

Haut Coulet 31
Herbiers, Hameau des 43
Hotel, Pension, Guesthouse:
  Auenerhof 120, 139
  Baur 154
  Bella Vista 127
  Ciurnadú 145, 146
  Cristol 36, 37
  Cube 115
  Cuntera 103
  Edelweiss 149, 152
  Eden 130
  Engstlenalp 92, 94-96
  Eggwirt 135
  Franzenshöhe 127
  Frohsinn 99, 100
  Guidon, Bivio 117
  Modern 5
  les Mottets 45
  Naturfreundehaus 89
  Odles 145
  Oeschinensee 82-84,
  Pellas 108
  Post 113
  le Prarion 38, 55-57
  Rivage 65, 68
  Rosenlaui 90
  Rütli 99
  Schwarzschmied 136
  Sporthotel, Pontresina 119
  Sporting, Levigno 123
  Steinbock, Ansatz zum 141
  Süsom 118
  Therm 177

Tré-la-Tête 38, 54-55
Ultnerhoff 132, 134
Victoria 91,
le Vieux Moulin 63
Waldheim 132
Hospitz la Cruzs 145
Hut, Hütte, Camona:
  Blüemlisalphütte 85
  Brogelshütte 144
  Büllelejochhütte 159
  Camona da Medel 93, 103-104
  Camona da Terri 93, 105-107
  Comichihütte 159
  Drei Shusterhütte 150, 154, 156
  Drei Zinnenhütte 158
  Etzlihütte 92, 100-102
  Gespaltenhornhütte 85
  Madritschhütte 131
  Medelserhütte 93, 103-104
  Rotstokhütte 87
  Samer Skihütte 139
  Schaubachhütte 131
  Schutzhütte Raschötz 120, 141, 143
  Senneshütte 148
  Staffelialp 92, 96-98
  Terrihütte 93, 105-107
  Zufallhütte 131

Ibex 46
Iffigenalp 69, 79-80
Inner Glas 111
Inergrub, hamlet 134
Inner Üschene, valley 83
Irrighe, village 172
Isola 2000 6, 18-20
Isola, village 19

Jacobsweg Gaubünden 100, 102-103
Juel sattel 145
Joch:
　Jungfrau Joch 88
　Madritschjoch 121, 125-131
　Oberbachernjoch 159
　Stilfser Joch 121, 125-126, 180
Jungfrau 69, 86, 90

Kandersteg, town 83, 181
Kaserfeld Alm 134
Kleine Scheidegg 88, 89
Klausen, town 141

Lac(s), Lago, lake(s):
　d'Anterne 59
　des Babarottes 25
　du Boréon 17
　di Cancano 125
　Cavillon 42
　di Centro Cadore 164
　di Colle di Santa Anna 21
　de Cristol 40
　du Diable 13
　Fourca 14
　Geneva 37, 63-73
　du Grattaleau 49
　Lausfer Inferieurs 21
　Lausfer Superieur 21
　de la Leisse 48-49
　di Livigno 124
　de Lovenex 70-71
　Lucerne 99
　de la Muta 14
　de la Plagne 49
　de Prals 15
　Premier 30
　de Roselend 54
　Rood 40
　de Roue 35
　Ste. Marguerite 42-43
　San Bernolfo 22
　de Sanetsch, Senein 76-77
　di San Giacomo di Faéle 125
　Santa Croce 171-172, 176
　de Taney 71-72
　de Tenechet 80
　du Trem 14
　del Vajont 167
　du Vallonnet Superieur 29
　de Vens 25-26
　Vert, day 26, 58
　Vert, day 28, 61
Lai da Marmorera 116
Lana Postal 133, 137, 182
Lance, hameau la 53
Lapista mountain restaurant 61
Lanches, mine works 51
Larche, village 26, 28-29
Lausanne port of Ochey 65, 68
Lauterbrunnen 69, 86-88
Leaderalm 138
Livigno tax free valley 121
Livingno, town 123-124
Loza la 45
Lumbrein, village 108

Madone de Fenestre 6, 14-16, 181
Maisons, Hameau les 35
Martagon Lilly 98
Martelltal, footpath 132
Mattes, Vacherie du 62
Meiringen, town 67-69, 90-94, 181
Menton, town 2, 5-7, 181
Meran, banhoff 133
Mercantour Natl. Park 11-28
Mercière, Tête, Col 18-19

Merveilles, Relais de 15
Mieux, village 72-73
Moar zu Tassis 142
Modane, town 43-44, 181
Mönch 86
Mont, le village 45
Mont, village 172
Mont Archas 18
Mont Blanc 38, 54-59
Mont:
  Giagiabella 9
  de Grange 62
  Mounier 21
  Pelve 47
  Pourri 38
  Thabor 38, 42
Montchavin, village 51
Monte:
  Cavallo 150, 171
  Ciastelin 150, 163
  Toc 167
  Pizzoc 175, 176
  Viso 6, 20, 26
Moos 135
le Moulin, village 51
Mourière, belvedere de 33
Morteratsch station 122
Mürren, village 87
Murtel, cable car station 118
Mutschnengia, village 92, 102-103

Nant Borant, village 55
Névache, Villes Basse 41
Névache, Ville Haute 37, 39-41
Nice Airport 18, 181
Niederdorf 120-121, 149-152
Niederdorf-Prags, station 181
Notre Dame du Charmaix 44
Novel, village 64, 70

Obereggen, farm 135
Obere Schäferhütte 128
Oberland, restaurant 88
Odel 144
Oeschinensee 69, 82-84
Ortler 120-121, 124-131
Ortler north ridge 128-129
Orsoligna, village 160

Palantina, Cabina ra 174
Parsonz, village 114
Pasque Flowers 12
Pas, Pass, Passo:
  Ammertepass 80-82
  Birkenschartl 154-155, 157-158
  de la Bosse 64
  del Bue 22
  du Boeuf 22
  de Cavale 27
  de Colle Longue 23
  Crüzlipass 102
  de la Couletta 29-30
  du Diable 12-13
  Diesrut 107
  Glasspass 111
  Greina 107
  dal Güglia 109-110
  Güner Lückli 113
  Hohtürli 84-85
  Jochpass 96-97
  Kreuzjoch 144
  de Lovenex 70-71
  Lunghin 117
  de Morgon 26-27
  di S Osvaldo 167
  Ste. Anne 21
  Sarlriedle 153
  Sefinefurgge 67, 86
  Septimerpass 117

Pas, Pass, Passo continued:
  Soyscharte 132
  la Stretta 122-123
  Surenenpass 98
  Umbrai, 126
  Usser Glas 111
  di Valle Alpisella 124
Pension see: Hotel, Guesthouse
Pescol, village 145
Peyrolle, Petite and Grand 38
Pian de Cansiglio 175
Pian Deibuoy 162
Pic d'Escreins 32
Pineda, hamlet 167
Piz Aul 92
Piz:
  Bernina 92-93, 118, 120, 122-123
  Caschenleglia 104-105
  Curver 92
  d'Err 92
  Güglia 92
  Gaglianera 106
  Medel 106
  Somplunt 145
Plan:
  des Eaux 50
  de la Lai, refuge 54
  de Lasta 148
  de Lyon 7
  des Roses 80
  des Sarens Alp 147
de la Planche, hameau 64
Planplatten ridge 94
Pleiv, hamlet 109
Pointe de Ventabren 11
Pont:
  de Châtelet 31
  du Countet 15
  de la Fonderie 42
  d'Ingolf 18

  des Nants 60
  de Sales 60
Pontresina 92-93, 119, 120-122
Portes de l'Hiver 61
Port de Cristol 40
Ports de Soleil, ski area 62
Pragser Wildsee 149
le Prarion 57
la Pré Premier 35
Primula Restaurant 161

Queyras, Alps 31-36
Queyras, Château 34

Refuge, cabane:
  Abricotine 61-62
  de l'Aiguille Doran 44
  d'Anterne Alfred Wills 38, 59
  de l'Arpont 38, 46
  des Audannes, cabane 69, 79
  la Balme 53
  de Basse Rua 32
  de Bise 64
  de Chambeyron 30
  du Col de la Croix du Bonhomme 55
  du Col du Palet 49
  d'Entre Deux Eaux 47
  Entre le Lac 38, 49-50
  de la Golèse 38, 60
  de la Leisse 38, 48
  la Madone de Fenestre 6, 15, 181
  des Merveilles 6, 14
  Moëde Anterne 58
  Monte Scale 125
  de Mont Thabor 38, 42
  de l'Orgère 44
  du Plan de la Lai 38, 54
  le Prarion 38, 56

Refuge continued
  Pre Alpini 42
  de Rosuel 50
  Tré-la-Tête 38, 55
  de Vens 6, 25
  la Vouivre 71
Reichenbach falls 91
Rhine-Danube watershed 117
Riom, town 114
Rifugio:
  Baion 162, 163
  Carducci 150, 159
  Casera Ditta 150, 167
  Ciareido 150, 161-162
  del Laus 6, 22
  Dolomieu al Dolada 150, 171
  Padova 150, 164
  Pordone 166
  San Osvaldo 175
  Semenza 150, 173
River, Rivière, Torrent:
  Abondance 63
  Alpbach 83
  Ammertebach 81
  Arc 44
  Arve 58
  Bévéra 10
  Clarée 40
  Dar 75
  Engleberger 97
  Etzlibach 101, 102
  Fossan 73
  Gelgia 114
  Glevieux 60
  Glogn 108, 109
  Grand Eau 73-75
  Guil 34
  Hinterrhein 112, 113
  Isère 51
  Kander 83
  Leisse 47

Mezas 168
Morge 64, 70
Rein Anterior 103
Rein da Medel 104
Rein Posteriur 113
Rein da Sumvitg 107
Reusse 99
Rhein, Rein 103
Rhône 73
Rocheure 47
Roseg, Ova da 119
Rüschbach 76
Sales 60
Simme 80-81
Stollabach 152
Strem 103
Ubaye 31
Ubayette 28
Rochers de Fiz 59
Roches de Chaudin 64
Roubion, valley 41
Rumantsch language 93

Sachas, village 36
Safien Plaz, village 110
Saghäuser, hamlet 153
Sales, Point de 59
Sallettes, Ancien Fort des 37
Salouf town 114
Samoëns, town 60
St Bruno Lily 42
St Bernard Lily 95
St Étienne de Tinée 6, 24
St Gertraud, village 120, 132
St Gingolph 38, 64-68, 181
St Leonhard, village 145
St Maria in der Schmelz 132
St Martin Vesubie 18, 181
St Moritz, in Ultnertal 134
St Pankraz 135-136

St Walberg, village 135
St Wendelin Kapelle 129
Ste Barbe, Chapel 34
San Bernolfo, Roca di 6
San Martino, village 172
Sanetsch, barrage 77
Santa Augusta, church of 176
Sarlkofel 153
Sarlsattle 153
Sarnthein, village 139
Savognin, town 92, 115
Schmieden, village 149, 152
Schreckhorn 96
Seitenbachschart 149
Sennesertal 149
Sentaro Alpago Natura 174
Seres, village 120, 151
Serre des Aigles 37, 39
Shilthorn, 87
Sils, halt & village 112
Sospel 6, 9, 181
Soyalm, pasture hut 87
Soyscharte 132
Spilboden, restaurant 87
Staffelialp, restaurant 92, 97-98
Stambecco 46
Staol di Plois, hamlet 172
Stauber waterfall 98
Steinbock 46
Stilfsler Joch 126-127
Südtyrol 127-159
Sugen Alp, 115
Suisridl 153
Sulden, village 120, 129-130
Sunnenseitnweg, 135
Sunseitnsteig 137
Surlej, Fuorcla 118
Surlej, village 92, 117-118, 181
Surovas, railway station 122
Sylvaplana, town 117

Tabia da Rin 161
-tal, see: Val, Valley
Taney, village 69, 71
Terassenweg 89
Termignon 46
Tête:
 de Plate Lombarde 29
 Mercière 19
 Rougnouse de la Guercha 22
Thusis 92, 111-112, 181
Tines, Gorges des 60
Titlis 92, 94, 97, 98
Toblacher See 154
Torrent see: River, Rivière, stream,
Total distance walked 3
Total height gained 3
Totenkirchl 140
Tour du Mont Blanc 55
Trafoi village 120 125
Tre Chime 158
Trübesee 97
Tschingellochtighore 83
Tunnel du Châtelard 58

Ucia Lavareia 147
Ultner Talweg 135-136
Ultnertal 133-136

Val, Valley, -tal:
 Abondance 62-63
 Alpisella 124
 d'Arade 165
 Arc 1, 43
 Bella 174
 Claret 49
 Crüzlital 102
 d'Empuonrame 14
 Engiadin 112
 d'Escreins 33

Val, Valley, -tal Continued:
  Etroite 42
  Etzlital 101
  da Fain 122
  de Fanes 146
  Forcola 125
  Gental 94
  Grande Gouilles 78
  Inner Üschene 83
  Maderanertal 100
  Madritschtal 131
  Martelltal 132
  Mezas 167
  Mulegna 115
  de Piera 174
  Plattas 103
  de Poorse 161
  Reichenbachtal 90
  Rezliberg 80
  da Rin 161
  Roseg 118
  Salatis 173
  Serenne 31
  Strem 103
  Sulden 129-130
  Sursés 114-117
  Talagona 164
  Tinée 24
  Ubaye 30-31
  Ubayette 28
  Waldnachter 99
Valezan, village 38, 51-52, 181
Vallesella 164
Valley Hostel 87
Vallon, Vallone:
  di Collalunga 23
  della Guercia 22
  Laugier 31
  du Lauzanier 28
  de la Leisse 47
  des Pelouses 33
  du Ponset 15
  della Sauma 22
  de Thorse 42
Vallorch, hamlet 175
Vanoise Alps 44-51
Vella, town 92, 108
Ventabren, Pointe de 11
Vers l'Eglise 75
Vierwald-Stättersee 99
Vevey, town 65, 181
Veia Surmirana 112-118
Via Alpina 84-99
Vieux Servoz, village 58
Villanders village 120, 141
Villanderer Alm 141
Viraysse, Baraquements de 29
Vittorio-Veneto 150, 176-177
Vöran, village 137
Vorder Stafel 97
Vouvry, town 72-73
Vrin, village 107-108

Walserweg 111, 112
Wasenegg, ridge 87
Wendenstöcke 94
Wendelin Kapelle 129
Wengen 82
Wetterhorn 86, 90, 94, 96
Wildhorn 67, 78,

Yvorne, village 69, 73-74, 181

Zalöner Hütta 110
Zicker 142
Zufallhütte 131
Zurfritsee 132

ABOUT THE AUTHOR

Ian MacLennan was born in the Highlands in 1939 and his mother introduced him to wandering in the remote Scottish Hills. They moved south to Surrey in 1945 after his mother had been widowed. He attended Guy's Hospital Medical School, where he joined the Climbing Club and started Alpine Climbing. In 1964 he qualified in Medicine and subsequently specialized in Academic Clinical Immunology. After 10 years in Oxford he moved to the University of Birmingham in 1979. There he headed Immunology until his "retirement" in 2005, since when he has been able to focus on research, without clinical and administrative distractions. In Birmingham he became a member of the Birmingham Medical Research Expeditionary Society. This has enabled him to visit the Alps, Himalaya and Andes with like-minded friends, who have a passion for the high hills and an interest in altitude medicine. His wife Pam, their two sons, two granddaughters and five grandsons all enjoy walking and climbing in the hills.

Printed in Poland
by Amazon Fulfillment
Poland Sp. z o.o., Wrocław